BestMasters

Mit **„BestMasters“** zeichnet Springer die besten Masterarbeiten aus, die an renommierten Hochschulen in Deutschland, Österreich und der Schweiz entstanden sind. Die mit Höchstnote ausgezeichneten Arbeiten wurden durch Gutachter zur Veröffentlichung empfohlen und behandeln aktuelle Themen aus unterschiedlichen Fachgebieten der Naturwissenschaften, Psychologie, Technik und Wirtschaftswissenschaften. Die Reihe wendet sich an Praktiker und Wissenschaftler gleichermaßen und soll insbesondere auch Nachwuchswissenschaftlern Orientierung geben.

Springer awards **“BestMasters”** to the best master’s theses which have been completed at renowned Universities in Germany, Austria, and Switzerland. The studies received highest marks and were recommended for publication by supervisors. They address current issues from various fields of research in natural sciences, psychology, technology, and economics. The series addresses practitioners as well as scientists and, in particular, offers guidance for early stage researchers.

Matthias Schaible

Decentralized Lending

Empirical Analysis of Interest and Liquidation Mechanisms

Springer Gabler

Matthias Schaible
Berlin, Germany

ISSN 2625-3577 ISSN 2625-3615 (electronic)
BestMasters
ISBN 978-3-658-39055-6 ISBN 978-3-658-39056-3 (eBook)
https://doi.org/10.1007/978-3-658-39056-3

Responsible Editor: Marija Kojic
This Springer Gabler imprint is published by the registered company Springer Fachmedien Wiesbaden GmbH, part of Springer Nature.
The registered company address is: Abraham-Lincoln-Str. 46, 65189 Wiesbaden, Germany

Preface

Without doubt, blockchain technology is one, if not the, key innovation in finance of the past years. By allowing for secure transactions without an intermediary, it has paved the way for further innovations such as smart contracts and decentralised finance (DeFi).

DeFi mainly refers to the practice of collateralised lending in cryptocurrencies, also referred to as peer-to-peer lending (P2P lending), where counterparty risk is mitigated by (i) collateral and (ii) smart contracts, which ensure execution of the agreed liquidation mechanism. These markets have grown tremendously in recent years, reaching a total-value-locked on the Ethereum blockchain of $100bn in October 2021 (Statista, 2022[1]).

This work will be extremely useful to readers seeking to get a head start in DeFi markets. By providing a comprehensive overview of DeFi markets, this work targets a business-oriented audience wishing to understand this vastly growing market. Matthias Schaible explains the different protocol layers comprising the DeFi architecture, the different applications of collateralised lending (e.g. leverage), the mechanisms of interest rate determination and the liquidation mechanisms. The empirical part revolves around the liquidations in response to price downturns. The author does not only explain the technical aspects in an understandable way, but also the financial components, such as the way users use collateralised lending to build a leveraged position.

[1] https://www.statista.com/statistics/1237821/defi-market-size-value-crypto-locked-usd/

I am convinced that this book will serve as a great reference for entering the world of DeFi.

Natalie Packham

Berlin
July 2022

Abstract

This paper deals with the concept of Decentralized Lending on the Blockchain. The aim of the paper is to provide an overview of how decentralized loans work and how the interest rates for them are composed. In addition, the empirical part of the thesis addresses the question of the extent to which price fluctuations of the deposited collateral have an influence on its liquidation.

In order to familiarize with the topic, the basic principles of the underlying technology, such as blockchain, smart contracts or the general architecture of Decentralized Finance, are highlighted. More specific points of Decentralized Lending, such as the principle of supplying and borrowing, lending pools and the underlying logic of overcollateralization will be presented in more detail subsequently. The various interest rate models are presented, and it emerges that the kinked rates model performs best in terms of counteracting the liquidity risk and avoiding high utilization.

The question of the extent to which price fluctuations of the deposited collateral have an impact on its liquidation is determined using data from the AAVE V2 lending platform. The crawling of the data from the blockchain posed a major challenge and is therefore presented in detail in this paper. With this data, it was possible to show that price fluctuations of collaterals are closely related to their liquidations; in particular, high negative rewards and high liquidations correlated strongly. Moreover, it was found that returns one hour before liquidation are a better measure than those at the time of liquidation, which is due to the fact that liquidations are purely a consequence of undercollateralization and must be addressed by liquidators in the network.

Contents

Abbreviations

BUSD	Binance USD
dApps	Decentralized Applications
DeFi	Decentralized Finance
DLT	Distributed-Ledger-Technology
ETH	Ethereum
EVM	Ethereum Virtual Machine
GUSD	Gemini Dollar
H_f	Health Factor
LINK	Chainlink
LP	Lending Pool
LT	Liquidation Threshold
LTV	Loan-to-Value
OLS	Ordinary Least Squares
P2P	Peer-to-peer
U	Utilization Rate
$U_{optimal}$	Optimal Utilization Rate
UNI	Uniswap
USDC	USD Coin
USDT	Tether
WBTC	Wrapped Bitcoin

List of Figures

List of Tables

Introduction

1

1.1 Background and Relevance of the Topic

In a world where it is possible to send messages and pictures for free, or even make long-distance video calls, the question arises why it is so much more difficult when it comes to sending money, offering loans or investing capital. With the introduction of Decentralized Finance (DeFi), these questions are to be addressed across the board in the future. DeFi describes an ecosystem of different layers, which are built on a blockchain, the so-called settlement layer, and will offer all forms of financial services in a decentralized manner. In contrast to today's financial world, which almost always requires an intermediary such as brokerages, exchanges, or banks to merge, establish trust and offer a financial instrument (Roth 2015), Decentralized Finance does not need such intermediary at all. Instead, DeFi is a financial infrastructure that uses smart contracts (Buterin 2013) and is built on blockchain-based software platforms, mostly the Ethereum Virtual Machine (EVM). The possible uses of smart contracts range from simple payments, through loans, to complex derivatives or general trading, where they act as a decentralized exchange (Grigo et al. 2020).

Many, especially new, DeFi projects face the challenge of constantly providing a certain amount of liquidity, which is needed to run the smart contracts, that hold the deposited tokens. This is provided by mortgaging crypto assets, which is surprising at first glance, since cryptos are primarily characterized by being flexible and more liquidity-oriented, in contrast to classic mortgaged assets such as real estate or annuities. But collateralized loans are probably the most common form of lending in Decentralized Finance. This means that a certain amount of money must be available in the user's account or other collateral must be proven before

M. Schaible, *Decentralized Lending*, BestMasters,
https://doi.org/10.1007/978-3-658-39056-3_1

a loan can be issued. Nevertheless, it can be worthwhile to deposit cryptocurrencies or stablecoins on these DeFi platforms. By doing so one can speculate with borrowed tokens and does not have to sell their own tokens while also profiting from the possessed token's price development while they are locked.

The interest rates of these decentralized applications (dApps), which are significantly higher than almost anything offered on the traditional financial market, show that the deposit of collateral alone is worthwhile, but also give an insight into the risks that are more exposed with this. The range for US dollar pegged stablecoins on established lending protocols is from 2.48% APY for USD Coin (USDC) on AAVE lending protocol (AAVE 2022) to 19.47% for TerraUSD (UST) on Anchor Protocol (Anchor Protocol 2022).

A look at the total value locked (TVL) of the three largest platforms shows that these are no longer small niche markets. As such, MakerDAO ($16.84 billion), AAVE ($10.62 billion), and Compound ($6.99 billion) collectively hold approximately $34.45 billion worth of tokens in their smart contracts (Defi-Pulse 2022)[1].

At first glance, this appears to be unusually high, but the underlying interest rate models are based on supply and demand in the relevant market, ensuring that there is always mathematical evidence. If deposited, the credit balance receives the interest mentioned above and can be used as collateral up to a certain Loan-to-Value (LTV), which describes the maximum borrowing power of a specific collateral. Depositing collateral thus not only adds liquidity to the protocol and grants the user an attractive interest rate, but also serves as creditor protection in the absence of real identities and KYC measures on lending protocols, by requiring the borrower to place collateral that is worth more than the value of the amount borrowed.

If the LTV is exceeded the credit position is considered unsecured and the collateral deposited must be liquidated. Liquidation therefore occurs when the value of the collateral falls below a certain liquidation threshold in relation to the borrowing, as a result of which the provided collateral is sold at a certain additional discount to cover the debt. For example, if collateral has a liquidation threshold of 80%, this means that the loan will be liquidated if the value of the debt is more than 80% of the value of the collateral (AAVE 2022). The most used application to take advantage of this construct is leveraging. The aim here is to achieve higher returns by increasing exposure to an asset. An example of increasing exposure to Ethereum (ETH):

---

[1] Stand 13/02/2022.

1. Supply ETH as collateral
2. Borrow USDC
3. Sell USDC for ETH
4. Repeat steps one to three

By repatriating the borrowed funds as collateral, a leverage spiral is built up that dramatically increases both exposure and risk of loss (Cousaert et al. 2021). Perez et al. (2021) found that on the compound lending platform 2,141 accounts with a total volume of about $600 million used the leveraged spiral technique, representing about half of the total funds added to the protocol at that time. Due to the high and erratic volatility within the crypto market, this can in practice, also in combination with the inflexibility of smart contracts, lead to a liquidation cascade being unleashed, which can quickly have a significant impact on the entire market. However, this Master's thesis will mainly address the problem of the influence of price fluctuations on the liquidation of deposited collateral, as this is the primary trigger for liquidations.

There are already some empirical analyses on the topic of liquidations in Decentralized Lending pools, but they mainly focus on high-level economic models or on the underlying mechanism, general risks or profitability of liquidations. There is no analysis of the extent to which fluctuations in the price of the underlying asset affect the liquidations of any of these assets. In addition, it is unclear whether liquidations are triggered exclusively by high price losses or whether liquidations also take place when prices are trending sideways or upwards. Also, interesting aspects like the involved smart contracts of the lending platforms, the structure of the DeFi architecture on the blockchain, and the composition of interest rates are also worth exploring in more detail.

1.2 Objective

The thesis objective can be derived from the observation of the increased interest in the topic of Decentralized Finance, especially decentralized loans, and the simultaneous lack of scientific publication. The specific objectives of this paper are the following:

1) It will be outlined how decentralized loans work in general and how the interest rates are composed, especially how supply and demand support the interest rates.

2) It will be empirically worked out to what extent price fluctuations of the deposited collateral have an influence on its liquidation.

To achieve objective 2), the different causes of liquidations will be identified and their frequencies, especially with regard to the behavior of the respective underlying, will be analyzed and the resulting consequences and their significance will be outlined.

1.3 Methodology

The theoretical basis for this work is provided by individual specialist literature, the majority of which is based on studies, research papers and various white papers. Relevant data were collected from scratch, as there is little academic research on decentralized loans. For this purpose, historical data from the Ethereum blockchain, as a publicly available database, has been crawled. Therefore, Covalent API (Covalent 2021a) authenticated the corresponding data via an API request from the blockchain. API stands for Application Programming Interface and is an interface that can be used to communicate with blockchain nodes. The requested data was transferred via REQBIN (REQBIN 2021) into a JSON format, converted from there into a csv and finally modeled in Excel and Gretl. Data collection, data cleansing and identification of relevant events took up the majority of the work here.

The data examined is on-chain data from AAVE V2 covering the period from January 1, 2021 to June 9, 2021, which was used to replicate the liquidation scenarios during the period in question. The data from the scenarios are examined primarily with regard to various correlations, trends and effects of liquidations using common quantitative methods such as regression analyses, two-means tests and two-proportion tests.

1.4 Structure of the Thesis

This Master's thesis provides an overview of Decentralized Lending on the blockchain before the empirical part deals with the central question of the extent to which liquidations are influenced by the price development of the deposited collateral. In order to answer this in a comprehensive and comprehensible way, chapter two provides a concise explanation of the theoretical foundations of blockchain technology. First, the functionalities of the blockchain itself, smart contracts as well as the DeFi architecture are described, which are essential for the use of Decentralized Lending, in order to provide a good understanding of the mechanisms.

Subsequently, the supply and borrow mechanisms in Decentralized Finance are shown and the application areas derived from them are explained. In addition, the various interest rate models of Decentralized Lending are presented and explained in more detail using the example of the AAVE lending platform.

Afterwards, the third chapter provides an empirical analysis of liquidations in relation to the price performance of the underlying collaterals on the AAVE lending platform for the period January to June 2021.

Chapter 4 finishes with the conclusion, in which the results are used to draw conclusions, the limitations of the study are highlighted and an outlook is provided.

2 Lending on the Blockchain

Despite all the critical sidetracks, SEC lawsuits, trading bans or other regulations, crypto's global market capitalization has more than tripled since January 2021 from about $776 billion to $2.7 trillion (Coingecko 2021).[1] Over the same period, total value locked (TVL) in DeFi protocols has increased fivefold from $25 billion to $101 billion (Defi-Pulse 2021a),[2] of which in turn just under 50% is attributable to the lending market (Defi-Pulse 2021b),[3] reflecting the growing interest and attractiveness of this market.

An elementary aspect added to the crypto market by DeFi is the possibility to generate income passively. This is achieved by means of staking, liquidity pools, yield farming or lending (Lau and Tse 2021; Kiong 2020), the latter of which is discussed in more detail in this paper. Besides the said possibility to earn money with Decentralized Lending, it is distinguished by the fact that it is permissionless (Werner et al. 2021), so anyone can interact with it and both lend and borrow. Furthermore, the peer-to-peer (P2P) approach avoids intermediaries and thus processing times and fees. In addition, the full backing of the loans by collateral, which must be provided in advance, ensures security and trust on the platforms, and also offers the possibility of leveraging. (Schär 2021). At the beginning of this chapter, the basics of blockchain and DeFi are explained, followed by a description of the mechanisms of Decentralized Lending.

[1] Status 25/10/2021.

[2] Status 25/10/2021.

[3] Status 25/10/2021.

Supplementary Information The online version contains supplementary material available at https://doi.org/10.1007/978-3-658-39056-3_2.

M. Schaible, *Decentralized Lending*, BestMasters,
https://doi.org/10.1007/978-3-658-39056-3_2

2.1 Basic Principles

In terms of Defi protocols, blockchains work as an underlying distributed ledger, without which the protocols cannot operate. These blockchains may be either a database, peer-to-peer network, or distributed ledger system, having the function of maintaining lists of transactions which have been confirmed by connected nodes, so-called mining nodes. They work without any third-party intermediary (Evans 2014; Swan 2015). Additionally, they are designed so they are able to provide consensus of which blocks are included. According to Perez (2020), Ethereum and Bitcoin make use of the so-called Proof-of-Work consensus. This consensus relies on miners, the actual block producers, solving highly advances computing puzzles, in order to generate new blocks.

2.1.1 Blockchain

Throughout the last decades the financial industry changed immensely. Especially since the global rise of cryptocurrencies the blockchain phenomenon has manifested its rightful place within the industry, with the financial sector being the primary user of the concept. This is due to the subject of considerable inefficiencies of processes and also matters of cost base in this industry. Blockchains as distributed ledgers act as a solution to these issues (Nofer et al. 2017). As the word suggests, in this kind of database data is stored in chains of blocks, with each encrypted block containing sets of data, including transaction records between two or more parties (Sherman et al. 2018). This storage process happens in chronological order, using cryptographic hashing and decentralization as a means for transparency and unchangeability of any data. This way, data is never copied, always accessible and transparent to the public, creating an irreversible record of any asset on the blockchain. This combination of features makes any blockchain tamperproof and secure (builtin.com 2021).

Though it seems like a fairly new phenomenon, the idea of blockchains has existed at least since the 1970s (Wong 1977). In his 1979 dissertation Ralph Merkle first introduced his idea of the Merkle hash tree, in which information can be linked in a tree-like structure. In the special case of a linear tree, information would then be chronologically chained (Merkle 1979). This idea was later adapted by Haber and Stornetta in 1990, using it as a time-stamp mechanism for documents (Haber and Stornetta 1991). However, these early prototypes of chaining information do not include any more advanced features of modern blockchains.

There are three core elements defining blockchain technology. First, blockchains appear as a distributed ledger, meaning a blockchain's decentralized nature. This is a significant advantage regarding security compared to centralized databases. While entries in said databases are secured by only one point of access through which every single entry may be attacked at once, each entry in a distributed ledger must be attacked individually for one information to be altered (Gans 2019). Additionally, the ledgers are constantly compared with one another to monitor and confirm alterations and additions (Cao et al. 2018). Of course, the downside to this security advantage are difficulties in scaling and adapting the ledger (Abadi and Brunnermeier 2018; Arrunada and Garicano 2018).

The second element is the virtual machine. As part of the blockchain architecture, the virtual machine is the engine for the decentralized network, as it provides the same computing resources to all participants in the network, thus working on top of the individual operating systems. Hence, the virtual machine may be referred to as a global processor for each participating computer in the network (Tara et al. 2019). While Bitcoin's virtual machine only allows for basic actions, Ethereum's is Turing complete, meaning it is able to perform any functions of conventional computers. Therefore, the Ethereum blockchain, for example, is able to automate different obligations, such as creating smart contracts, significantly reducing monitoring costs (Gans 2019).

The final core elements is the token. Cryptographic tokens represent digital assets, which are interchangeable and tradeable within their respective blockchain. They are always limited to one entry at a time and may be used as currencies within the blockchain, especially as rewards of developers. However, tokens are primarily used to distribute data within the network, as a means of communications (Gans 2019; Sherman et al. 2018).

As the first blockchain developed, Bitcoin's may be used to exemplify the work mechanism more in-depth, as shown in Figure 2.1. The core concept of this blockchain is to enable monetary transactions without using a financial institution. This is called peer-to-peer. Each transaction is time-stamped by hashing, creating a continuous proof-of-work, thereby outpacing possible attackers. To ensure that tokens are not used twice or have been altered respectively, each participating computer, the so-called nodes, must agree with the record of the existing chain. In practice, the network follows several steps of confirmation. First, any new transactions are presented to all nodes. The nodes then gather these data into a bundle, the actual block. A node will then work out complicated computational problems to create a proof-of-work for its specific block before presenting the block to all nodes (Nakamoto 2008; Nofer et al. 2017). This is followed by a validation process, which works on a consensus mechanism in which a majority of nodes need to agree on the validity of a transaction, therefore, reaching an "agreement on the state of a ledger" (Swanson 2015). Finally, the specific datablock is hashed and added to the chain (Nakamoto 2008; Nofer et al. 2017).

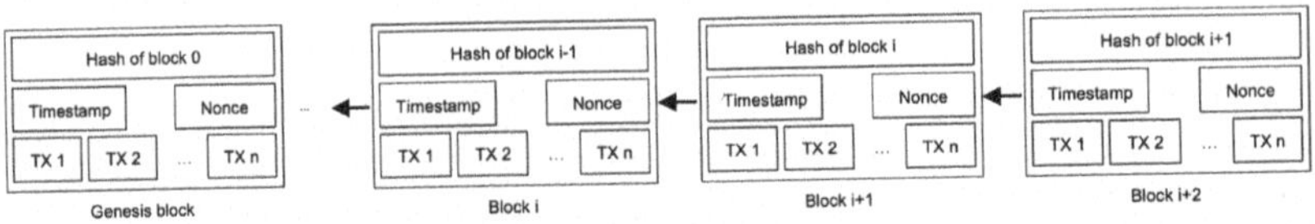

Figure 2.1 Example of a blockchain. (Own representation according to Zheng et al. 2016)

It Is notable, however, that the proof-of-work consensus used on Bitcoin's and Ethereum's blockchains is not applicable to all blockchains. There is a variety of possible control policies defining different kinds of blockchains. The afore mentioned mechanism defines permissionless blockchains, meaning notably anyone may potentially add to the chain. Permissioned blockchains, such as Corda 2016 or Hyperledger Fabric 2016, make use of a specified body who controls all transactions and alterations. Private and consortium blockchains are both types of permissioned blockchains. For the former control is provided by one single organization, while the latter relies on a group of organizations. Additionally, permissioned systems are usually faster and therefore less energy and time-consuming than permissionless blockchains (Sherman et al. 2018).

Besides all advantages blockchains may have, there are also challenges and problems regarding topics such as confidentiality, anonymity, accountability, and indelibility as well as technical long-term choices and developments such as security matters. Concerning technological matters, blockchains are responsible for immense energy consumption. This is especially true for blockchains using a proof-of-work computation, such as Bitcoin. Additionally, the rapid growth of ledgers and therefore transaction and processing time intensifies this problem (Sherman et al. 2018).

Moreover, blockchain technology and federal security laws correspond with each other. For instance, according to the "right to be forgotten" by the European Union the removal of personal data must be guaranteed to every person (Regulation (EU) 2016/679 (65)). This is especially complicated regarding ineradicable blockchains (Sherman et al. 2018).

2.1.2 Smart Contracts

Besides the blockchain itself, smart contracts are the second important component of Defi, as they define a set of rules that can be invoked by any other network participant. A smart contract is executable code running on a transaction-based blockchain to facilitate, execute, and enforce the terms of an agreement. The very purpose of a smart contract is to automatically execute the relevant terms of an agreement, but only when the conditions specified for doing so have been met (Alharby and van Moorsel 2017).

A smart contract consists of an account state, a private storage, and executable code. The contract's storage and account balance reflect the current status of the contract. Each time the smart contract is executed, the current status is updated and stored on the underlying blockchain. Figure 2.2 depicts the schematic of a decentralized cryptocurrency system with smart contracts. Usually, the storage file of a smart contract is implemented into the blockchain. Therefore, the network of miners can then implement the program and its prepositions, reaching agreement on actions and consequently updating the blockchain. Whenever the underlying code of a contract is contacted by a user or other contract it is automatically executed, reading from or writing to the according storage file. Additionally, smart contracts are able to interact with other contracts or users by receiving or sending money or storing cryptoassets. Regarding these assets, the contract acts as a "custodian". This means that the contracts automatically execute preset individual protocols on when, how and to whom an asset may be released. Consequently, smart contracts are the basis for innovative applications on blockchains (Schär 2021).

The idea of smart contracts was first established by Szabo (1994) and Miller (1997). According to Szabo (1997), preset agreements could be "embedded in the hardware and software we deal with, in such a way as to make a breach of contract expensive [...] for the breacher."

Because of an insufficient number of implementable systems, the only possibility to realize smart contracts was the progress of blockchain technology and the release of Ethereum (Buterin 2013) and other smart contract platforms (Wood 2021). Here, Ethereum can be seen as an extension of the Bitcoin blockchain, as a broader range of applications has not only been offered, but also made usable.

In conjunction with smart contracts, blockchain technology makes it possible to enter contracts using cryptography and without the involvement of intermediaries (Fairfield 2014).

Regarding the application of smart contracts in blockchains they operate on much more complex instructions than the simple buy/sell directives. By definition,

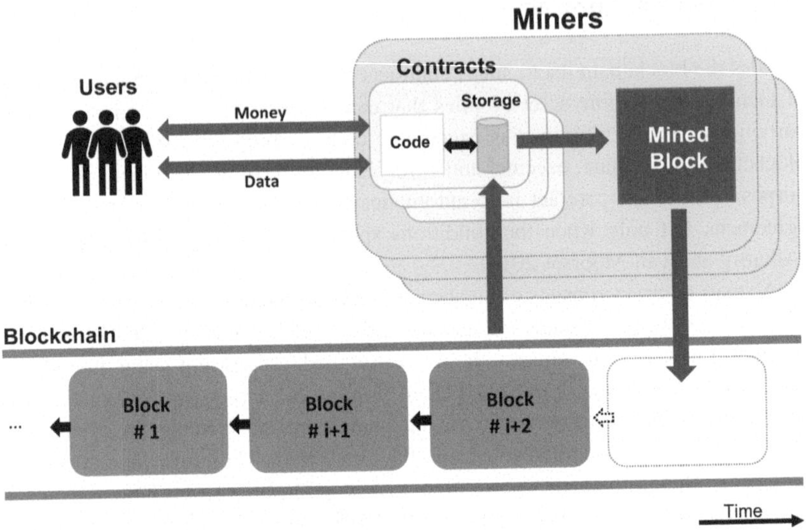

Figure 2.2 Decentralized cryptocurrency system with smart contracts. (Own representation according to Delmolino et al. 2016)

contracts include agreements by two or more parties to do or not do something and something else offered in exchange, whereby the parties need to be able to fully trust each other's promise to reach all obligations. Smart contracts operate with the same principle, using the underlying's token to form these agreements through the blockchain. However, trust is not a necessary component of a smart contract due to the code defining and executing a contract and, therefore, bypassing any human interventions, and also due to the public accessibility of the code (Swan 2015). This means that no matter the circumstances of each party the code will execute its protocol.

This could be good or bad depending on the situation, which is taken up again in the further course of the paper.

In fact, three elements of smart contracts that make them distinct are autonomy, self-sufficiency, and decentralization. A contract is autonomous in regard to not needing further maintenance once it is launched. Secondly, the self-sufficiency of a smart contract refers to the self-management of resources, and thus raising funds and reinvesting them on properties such as storage or processing power.

Third, smart contracts are decentralized in that they do not subsist on a single centralized server; they are distributed and self-executing across network nodes.

Information and content that does not exist natively on-chain is integrated into the virtual machines of the blockchains with the help of so-called oracles and read out there by smart contracts. Oracles are third party data feeds that have access to off-chain data, such as the ETH/USD exchange rate, through a mechanism (Perez et al. 2021), and an auxiliary service for most DeFi protocols (AAVE 2020; MakerDAO 2021; Leshner and Hayes 2019). Since the correctness of off-chain data cannot be verified once it has been fed in, trust in the oracle provider is needed on the one hand, and an incentive must be created for reporting as accurately and honestly as possible on the other, which is usually done by distributing corresponding tokens from the asset layer (Werner et al. 2021). However, there is still an oracle manipulation risk as well as certain disadvantages of third party off-chain data providers.

2.1.3 DeFi Architecture

To bring together the different components of blockchain and smart contracts, DeFi uses a so-called multi-layered architecture (Schär 2021). Each of these hierarchically superimposed layers has its own specific role to play. Amler et al. (2021) elaborated that the implementation of each DeFi function is the result of the interactions and transactions among the layers. In this architecture, the extent to which a layer is scalable, decentralized or vulnerable always depends on the underlying layer and ultimately the underlying blockchain. For example, if a permissioned ledger is used as the settlement layer, all decentralization efforts on the layers built on top of it would be ineffective (Xu et al. 2017), as the specific access rules mean that not everyone can interact with it.

Following on from this, figure 2.3 shows the Schär model, which refers to the Ethereum blockchain and distinguishes between five different layers.

The settlement layer, the bottom layer, is the blockchain used and the associated protocol asset, in this case Ether (ETH) for the Ethereum blockchain. It contains the basic operating rules of the ecosystem and is therefore the backbone of DeFi, as all other layers are based on it. On this public blockchain, all ownership information is stored, and the native currency is used to carry out the transactions of the dApps, which makes the security and trust of the underlying just as important as its scalability and the gas fees incurred.

This is the basis for the asset layer, which consists of all assets that can be issued on the settlement layer. This includes the native protocol value, but also stablecoins or Non-Fungible Tokens (NFTs). Tokenization denotes the process of adding new assets to a blockchain. Roth, Schär, and Schöpfer (2019) show that there are several ways to set up tokens on a blockchain, with the great majority being set up on the Ethereum blockchain via smart contract templates, the so-called ERC-20 token standard. The number of ERC-20 tokens that have contracts on the Ethereum blockchain as of October 2021 is close to 460,000 (Etherscan 2021), which is a clear indicator of the popularity of Ethereum as an underlying, also in view of a 31% increase since January 2021 (Schär 2021). Out of the top 2,000 tokens, 50% are backed by Ethereum, which in turn accounts for 73% of the market capitalization, again highlighting Ethereum's leading role as a settlement layer and thus its influence on the asset layer (attachment 1).

The protocol layer sets standards for specific use cases such as decentralized exchanges, debt markets, derivatives, and asset management via smart contracts. The standards defined here can be accessed and used simultaneously by multiple entities, ensuring interoperability across the entire architecture.

The application layer is the actual face of DeFi that users get to see. It houses the dApps, which make the underlying protocols available to the user as services. For example, applications such as decentralized exchanges or lending services can be found on this layer, which means that it not only has to pick up on the technical capabilities of its underpinnings but should also offer a web browser-based front-end interface for the mainstream (Katona 2021).

The aggregation layer is the final layer in the DeFi tech stack and can be seen as an extension of the application layer, as this is where aggregators connect various applications from the previous layer together in a user-centric platform. This provides the user with tools and services that gather relevant information from the protocols and helps in the seamless circulation of money between the different financial instruments, allowing the user to combine the benefits of different DeFi applications, as pointed out by Schär (2021).

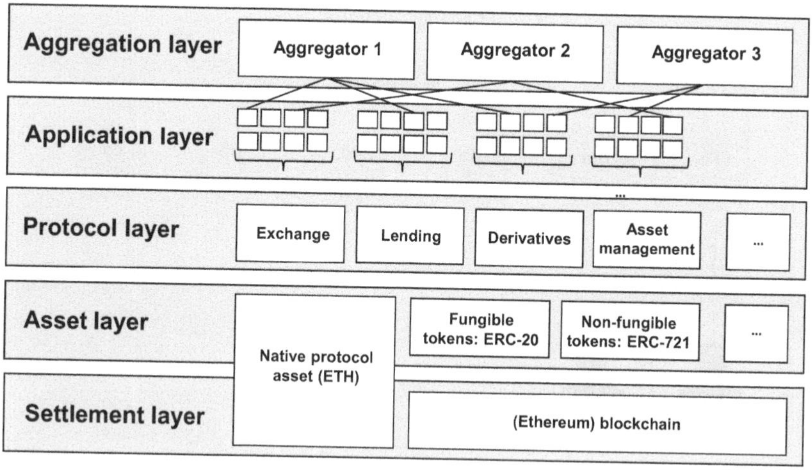

Figure 2.3 Schär model of a Decentralized Finance stack. (Own representation according to Schär 2021)

2.2 Supplying and Borrowing in Decentralized Lending

In order to be able to explain the principle of supplying and borrowing in DeFi, it is recommended to first take a look at the whitepapers of the leading lending pool platforms, namely AAVE, Compound and MakerDAO (AAVE 2020; Leshner and Hayes 2019; MakerDAO 2021). In contrast to classic P2P lending, where loans are granted directly between lenders and borrowers, the dApps rely on a pool-based strategy, which has the advantage that lenders do not have to create, manage and monitor loan offers and both lenders and borrowers remain anonymous (Leshner and Hayes 2019).

In this pool-based strategy, the user transfers his tokens, or if possible, his Fiat money, to a so-called lending pool (LP), which is an application that uses smart contracts to create a market. The AAVE whitepaper (2020) describes LPs as a collection of different currencies into which lenders can deposit and borrowers can withdraw. Unlike peer-to-peer lending, funds are pooled so that one lender can lend to a number of borrowers and vice versa. Figure 2.4 describes this process as an example, where user A has deposited ETH and user B DAI, i.e., they both add liquidity to the pool, but only user A also acts as a borrower by borrowing DAI.

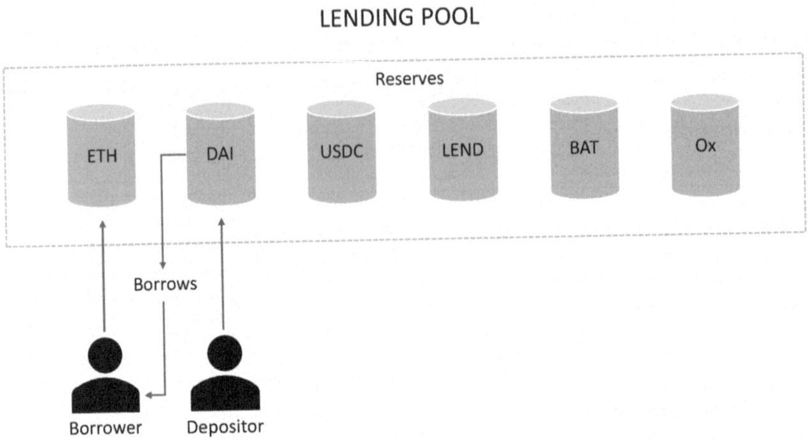

Figure 2.4 Lending pool principles. (Own representation according to AAVE 2020)

In Decentralized Lending there are two ways to borrow: Overcollateralized loans and Flash Loans. A classic example of an overcollateralized loan is the purchase of a property. In order to protect against possible loan defaults, the lender in most cases requires that the property to be purchased be pledged as collateral for the loan, whereby the loan only amounts to between 70 and 90 percent of the net asset value of the property - the loan is thus overcollateralized.

One advantage of crypto, namely anonymity, becomes a major disadvantage when it comes to granting credit, since neither identity nor credit score is given. To protect lenders and ensure the trust needed for a loan transaction, potential borrowers must first deposit collateral in an LP in order to cover the value of the debt (Qin et al. 2021). In addition to creating trust, overcollateralization also serves as a buffer against price fluctuations in the volatile crypto market.

The amount that can be lent for the deposited collateral depends on the asset deposited in the LP, as each has its own LTV. For this purpose, the weighted average of the different LTVs of the currencies constituting the collateral is used, with the weight for each LTV corresponding to the equivalent value of the collateral, for which the underlying native protocol asset is mostly used, for example in the case of AAVE it is ETH (AAVE 2020).

If the maximum LTV is reached, some lending platforms will liquidate the loan immediately (Leshner and Hayes 2019), while others will not allow to borrow new funds, but still have a small buffer before liquidation (AAVE 2020), which is a kind of safety leeway in which the users still have the possibility to add collateral or to (partially) repay the loan. The point at which the loan is liquidated once it exceeds this is called the liquidation threshold (LT), which is set individually for each asset according to the LTV approach. The following example exemplifies the borrowing process.

1. Deposit 10 ETH as collateral (75% LTV; 80% LT)
2. Borrow any asset to a maximum amount of 7.5 ETH
3. The borrow position now must have a health factor $H_f > 1$ at all times

The health factor H_f is the numeric representation of the safety of the deposited assets against the borrowed assets and its underlying value (AAVE 2020; Castro-Iragorri et al. 2021). It can be described with the following function:

$$H_f = \frac{\sum Collateral \times LT}{\sum Borrowed + Fees} \tag{2.1}$$

If $H_f < 1$, the loan is considered undercollateralized and the liquidation process begins (see chapter 3).

Loans are granted for an indefinite period of time, with interest accruing each Ethereum block added to the loan amount. In addition, the loan is not subject to a repayment schedule, for example with a fixed annuity, but can be repaid in full or in part at any time (Bavosa 2020), whereby it is only considered to have been repaid when both the amount granted, and the interest accrued have been refunded (Qin et al. 2021a).

Flash loans, on the other hand, are instant loans that are granted without any collateral and must be repaid in the same Ethereum transaction (Kulechov 2021). This is made possible by the Ethereum Virtual Machine's ability to set so-called checkpoints and roll back transactions if certain conditions are not reached (Gudgeon et al. 2020a; Ethereum Foundation 2020). Flash Loans are processed via smart contracts, where the user only needs to have enough funds on his wallet to pay the transaction fees. The requested flash loan is made available to the user's requesting smart contract and can subsequently be used for various actions within the term of the transaction. The possible uses range from various arbitrage concepts to debt refinancing and debt/collateral swaps, which will be discussed in more detail in the next chapter.[4]

---

[4] The applications for flash loans differ from overcollateralized loans in certain respects and in some cases also create other possibilities, but this is negligible for this thesis.

2.3 Applications

Decentralized Lending offers users a wide range of possible applications.

In addition to traditional borrowing for consumption, these are mainly investment strategies that can reflect the full range of the risk-return tradeoff, and the most relevant ones are briefly presented below.

2.3.1 Simple Lending

In times of collective zero interest rates on conventional savings, DeFi offers a way out by earning attractive interest on locked-in amounts. The easiest way to do this is to act as a lender by depositing your assets in LPs and thereby generating revenue from the loan interest as well as governance tokens, which are distributed according to the platform (Simon et al. 2021).

Here the user gets interest for his deposited amount and at the same time participates in the performance of his asset, because he did not have to sell it.

2.3.2 Arbitrage

Since there are price differences between the various exchanges, this provides an opportunity for arbitrageurs to borrow an asset on one platform and sell it at a higher price on another. The process follows the same pattern as arbitrage trading with currencies or shares, except that cryptocurrencies or stablecoins are used as assets here and a collateral is deposited first.

1. Borrow (crypto-) asset XYZ
2. Sell XYZ on exchange A for P_A
3. Buy XYZ on exchange B at P_B with $P_B < P_A$

It is worth noting that $\Delta P * q$ must be larger than the spent gas fees, which, especially at peak times on ETH, can quickly go into the hundreds of dollars, to make a profit. This can be achieved by trading high amounts, since the gas fee is paid per transaction regardless of the amount, or by reducing the gas price, which moves you down the miners' priority list and takes waiting time (Wang et al. 2021; YCharts 2021). Alternatively, switch to a network with low gas fees, such as Polygon, Wanchain, or Avalanche, which does not (yet) have Ethereum's offerings.

2.3.3 Leveraging

In Decentralized Lending, the collateral deposited can also be used for leveraging, with the aim of achieving higher returns through increased exposure to an asset. As explained earlier, in Decentralized Lending the borrower first slips into the role of lender by depositing his funds in an LP, where he can in turn use what he has borrowed as collateral and thereby borrow more again (Perez et al. 2021). In this so-called margin trading, both short and long positions can be taken.

In a short position, an asset is borrowed with the assumption that it will decrease in value. Therefore, the position is sold directly in order to buy it back at a lower price in the future (Gudgeon et al. 2020b). At best, a stablecoin pegged to the dollar is used as collateral to avoid exposure to volatility on this side of the position. If, on the other hand, profits are to be maximized, an asset that is expected to increase in value is used as collateral. This approach is associated with significantly more risk, because if the asset should lose value against expectations and the H_f should fall below one, liquidation is imminent.

In the following, the leverage process of a short position is shown, whereby this can be repeated as often as desired until the new borrowed amount tends towards zero at the latest:

1. Supply USDC as collateral
2. Borrow ETH
3. Sell ETH for USDC
4. Repeat steps one to three

The same principle can be applied to a long position to profit from the increase in value of an asset. In this case, the borrower wants to increase his exposure in an asset, whereby he at best contributes this asset directly as collateral, because in contrast to the short position, stablecoins are borrowed here in order to profit from their value stability on the credit side. The borrowed stablecoins are used to buy the asset to be leveraged, which is then used as collateral again, and so on as shown below:

1. Supply ETH as collateral
2. Borrow USDC
3. Sell USDC for ETH
4. Repeat steps one to three

As already mentioned, assets in an LP can only be leveraged up to a certain LTV, which in turn means that leveraging is in praxis not infinite and only possible at a decreasing rate. Thus, the total debt can be calculated by the following formula:

$$D = \left(\sum\nolimits_{i=1}^{k} \frac{\alpha}{\delta}\right) \times (1 + \gamma) \quad (2.2)$$

where α describes the collateral deposited, k the leverage factor and γ the interest rate. δ is the collateralization ratio, which is calculated from the LTV $\left(\delta = \frac{1}{LTV}\right)$ and indicates how much collateral must be deposited for the asset to be lent $\left(C = \frac{D}{\delta}\right)$. Note that equation (2.2) assumes that all loans for the same asset are taken out in the same LP at the same collateralization ratio, making the interest rate applicable to all loan positions. How interest rates come about and what they mean for Decentralized Lending will be examined in more detail in the next chapter.

2.4 Interest Rate Models

The interest rate is the price of money. Following this principle from the traditional world of finance, in Decentralized Lending market supply and demand also determine the interest rate (Saengchote 2021). Since the objective of LPs is to earn enough interest on borrowers to pay depositors, the interest rates of the deposited funds are a mirror image of the respective supply and demands. According to Gudgeon et al. (2020b), the underlying mechanism that determines the condition of the equilibrium to be achieved is key in shaping the whole protocol and ultimately the interest rates. In the context of LPs, the interest rate setting mechanism is encoded at the protocol level of the architecture in smart contracts where it is set or can be adjusted as part of a governance process (Castro-Iragorri et al. 2021).

The different credit protocols can be distinguished according to the interest rate model chosen. A distinction can be made between variable and stable interest rates models, whereby the variable interest rate models can in turn be divided into linear, non-linear, and kinked models (Gudgeon et al. 2020b). What they all have in common is that they base their calculation of interest on the utilization rate U (U = *Total Borrows / Total Supply*), describing which share of the LPs total capital is borrowed at time t (Cousaert et al. 2021). $U = 0$ describes a state of "under-utilization", in which there is no demand for the funds provided and interest rates are therefore low. As the utilization rate gets closer to 1, the capital becomes scarcer until no more liquidity is available when $U = 1$. While this status leads to quite high interest rates in order to be attractive to potential lenders and unattractive to potential borrowers on the one hand, it also creates a liquidity risk on the other. This liquidity risk is noticeable in the fact that if more funds are to be withdrawn from the LP than it has available liquidity, not all orders can be fulfilled.

2.4.1 Linear Rates Model

A linear interest rate model is an equation that describes a relationship between two quantities, in this case interest and utilization rate, that have a constant rate of change. The borrowing interest rates i_b are determined in a market for loans m as follows:

$$i_{b,m} = \alpha + \beta U_m \tag{2.3}$$

whereby α describes a per-block base rate and β is a slope coefficient for the dependence of the borrowing rate on the utilization rate. To make the interest rate spread ($i_{b,m}$ - $i_{s,m}$) positive, the savings interest rate i_s scales the interest rate $i_{b,m}$ by U_m as shown in the following equation:

$$i_{s,m} = (\alpha + \beta U_m)U_m \tag{2.4}$$

A small portion of this spread is allocated to a reserve pool, which is intended to minimize the pool's liquidity risk in times of low liquidity (Perez et al. 2021).

2.4.2 Non-linear Rates Model

The linear curve already rewards lenders for providing a scarce asset in times of need. The non-linear curve goes beyond this by increasing the interest rate non-linear the closer the event $U = 1$ approaches (Juliano 2017; dYdX 2019). This results in the following nonlinear model for the borrowing rates i_b in a market for loans m, where γ is another slope coefficient:

$$i_{b,m} = (\alpha \times U_m) + \left(\beta \times U_m^{32}\right) + \left(\gamma \times U_m^{64}\right) \tag{2.5}$$

whereas the saving interest rate i_s is as follows:

$$i_{s,m} = (1 - \lambda) \times i_{b,m} \times U_m. \tag{2.6}$$

λ indicates the reserve factor of the LP involved.

2.4.3 Kinked Rates Model

The most commonly used interest rate model on the leading lending platforms is the so-called kinked interest model, which has the special feature that the rate changes sharply as soon as a certain threshold value is exceeded or undershot (AAVE 2021b; Compound 2020). In order to better counteract the liquidity risk and avoid high utilization, the interest rate curve is kinked at the point of the optimal utilization rate $U_{optimal}$. For example, if $U_{optimal} = 80\%$ is set, the yield curve rises slowly with increasing utilization (borrowing). If the 80% limit is exceeded, i.e., if more than 80% of the LP liquidity is lent, the yield curve bends and rises rapidly to make further liquidity withdrawals unattractive and repayments / increases in liquidity attractive. The aim is to push the utilization rate of the LP below $U_{optimal}$ as quickly as possible.

The borrowing rates i_b can be characterized as follows:

$$i_b = \begin{cases} \alpha + \beta U & if\ U \leq U_{optimal} \\ \alpha + \beta U_{optimal} + \gamma(U - U_{optimal}) & if\ U > U_{optimal} \end{cases} \tag{2.7}$$

Again, α represents the base rate and β the multiplier per-block. U describes the utilization rate at time t and γ denotes the jump multiplier, which provides the kink.

Assets that are mainly used as collateral and therefore require a higher level of liquidity are usually issued with a $U_{optimal}$ of around 45% (AAVE 2021b).

By equation (2.8), the associated savings interest rates are given:

$$i_s = U(i_b(1 - \lambda)) \tag{2.8}$$

The supply rate is mitigated by U, as already described for the linear and non-linear models, because there must be enough revenue to pay off depositors, and the reserve factor λ sets aside interest income as a buffer against potential credit risk for the particular LP.

2.4.4 Stable Rates Model

On some lending platforms users are given the option to choose between variable and stable interest rates. A prominent example of this is AAVE, whose whitepaper is used below to explain the composition of the stable rate model.[5]

In contrast to variable interest rates, stable interest rates have the advantage of longer-term planning security. However, this planning certainty comes at the price of an interest rate premium, which is two to three times the variable interest rate. For example, while the variable borrowing rates for USDC are 3.98%, the stable rates are 10.99% (Aavewatch 2021).[6]

It is also worth mentioning that the stability of interest rates is not guaranteed over a specific term, but only until the rebalancing conditions are met (AAVE 2021b). These rebalancing conditions are, first, a utilization rate in the borrowed asset of $U_t > 95\%$ and, second, the total reserve lending ratio R_O, which is calculated as a weighted average between total variable loans and total stable loans, which must be overall $R_O > 25\%$.

The stable borrowing rate $i_{b,s}$ is based on the following equation:

$$R_s^t = \begin{cases} M_r + \frac{U}{U_{optimal}} R_{slope1} & if\ U \leq U_{optimal} \\ M_r + R_{slope1} + \frac{U - U_{optimal}}{1 - U_{optimal}} R_{slope2} & if\ U > U_{optimal} \end{cases} \tag{2.9}$$

where M_r serves as the base rate and is derived from the arithmetic mean of the total borrowed funds. R_{slope1} denotes the interest rate slope below U and R_{slope2} the interest rate slope above U. It should be noted that R_s^t is only calculated at time t and only affects newly opened positions, not existing positions with stable rates.

2.5 Influence of the Utilization Rate on the Interest Rate

The most important interest rate mechanisms were presented, of which only the variable rates are currently relevant, as they account for a lending market share of 98% at AAVE (Frangella 2020) and even more in the overall market, since AAVE is currently the only relevant provider offering stable rates.

[5] The following equations are not universal but refer to the borrowing rates i_b in the stable rates model of AAVE (AAVE 2020).

[6] Status 10/11/2021.

Figure 2.5 shows the different yield curves based on the variable models discussed using the variable interest rate model parameters for USDC given by AAVE (2021a). What is striking here is that the kinked interest rate behaves like a linear interest rate up to $U_{optimal}$. At $U = 89\%$, the difference between the two is only 0.4% in interest, whereas at $U = 91\%$ it has already increased to 6.36%, which, as previously discussed, serves to protect against liquidity risk. It also becomes clear why the kinked interest rate is the preferred model of the leading lending platforms. While the linear model does not offer any preventive protection against liquidity risk, with the non-linear model the target interest rates already rise to over 5% at $U = 51\%$, which means that a large part of the available pool liquidity remains unused, as the users expose themselves to an increasingly higher interest rate risk as the utilization rate increases. As a result, LPs using a non-linear interest rate model would have to have a significantly higher liquidity volume than LPs with kinked interest rates in order to be able to compete with their interest rates.

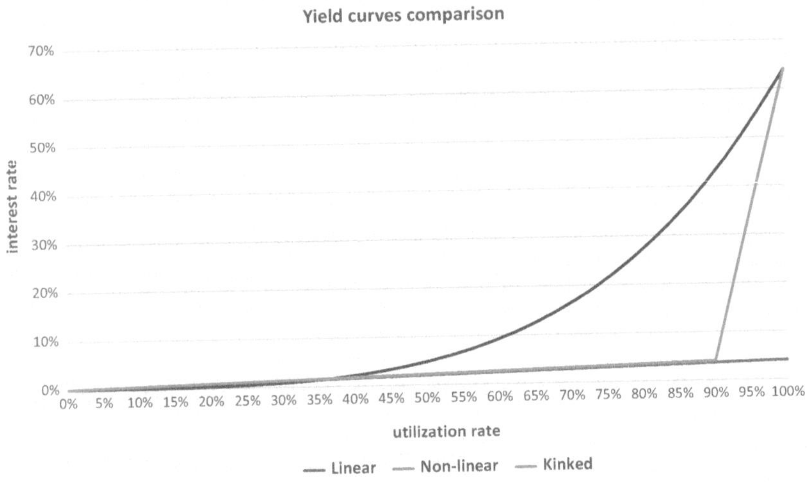

Figure 2.5 Modeled yield curves using USDC as an example. (Own representation)

In addition to the already explained utilization rate, the composition of the interest rates for the individual assets also includes $U_{optimal}$, M_r, R_{slope1} and R_{slope2}. Table 2.1 shows the parameters given for this purpose, which are calculated according to asset clusters with similar risk profiles.

These clusters mainly distinguish between stablecoins (AMPL-USDT) and other assets (BAL-ZRX). Since the mostly dollar pegged stablecoins are significantly less volatile and also less used as collateral, they are granted a higher $U_{optimal}$ (AAVE 2021b). The base rate is 0% by default (AAVE 2020), with the exception of SNX, as the Synthetix platform offers particularly high staking incentives (AAVE 2021). The significantly higher R_{slope1} and R_{slope2} numbers of the assets compared to the stablecoins are noteworthy, which makes them react much more sensitively to changes in U and also causes the yield curve to rise more sharply when $U_{optimal}$ is exceeded. An exception is AMPL, whose R_{slope1} is only half as high as the rest of the stablecoins, whereas R_{slope2} exceeds them by at least a factor of 100. This, in conjunction with the lower $U_{optimal}$, suggests that AMPL is to be prevented from becoming illiquid.

Table 2.1 Variable interest rate parameters. (Own representation according to AAVE 2021b)

Asset	$U_{optimal}$	Base rate	R_{slope1}	R_{slope2}
AMPL	75.00%	0.00%	2.00%	10000.00%
BUSD	80.00%	0.00%	4.00%	100.00%
DAI	80.00%	0.00%	4.00%	75.00%
GUSD	80.00%	0.00%	4.00%	100.00%
PAX	90.00%	0.00%	4.00%	60.00%
RAI	80.00%	0.00%	4.00%	75.00%
sUSD	80.00%	0.00%	4.00%	100.00%
TUSD	80.00%	0.00%	4.00%	75.00%
USDC	90.00%	0.00%	4.00%	60.00%
USDT	90.00%	0.00%	4.00%	60.00%
BAL	45.00%	0.00%	7.00%	300.00%
BAT	45.00%	0.00%	7.00%	300.00%
CRV	45.00%	0.00%	7.00%	300.00%
ENJ	45.00%	0.00%	7.00%	300.00%
ETH	65.00%	0.00%	8.00%	100.00%
KNC	65.00%	0.00%	8.00%	300.00%
LINK	45.00%	0.00%	7.00%	300.00%
MANA	45.00%	0.00%	7.00%	300.00%
MKR	45.00%	0.00%	7.00%	300.00%
REN	45.00%	0.00%	7.00%	300.00%
REP	45.00%	0.00%	7.00%	150.00%
SNX	80.00%	3.00%	12.00%	100.00%
UNI	45.00%	0.00%	7.00%	300.00%
WBTC	65.00%	0.00%	7.00%	100.00%
XSUSHI	45.00%	0.00%	7.00%	300.00%
YFI	45.00%	0.00%	7.00%	300.00%
ZRX	45.00%	0.00%	7.00%	300.00%

Table 2.2 compares the top10 assets by total supply on AAVE. It is noticeable that the utilization rate for stablecoins is quite close to $U_{optimal}$, while only marginal amounts are lent out for the assets. It can be concluded that assets such

as ETH or WBTC[7] are preferably used as collateral to borrow stablecoins that are resistant to price volatility, which is supported by the findings of Saengchote (2021), who found that 89% of loans on Compound are issued in stablecoins. This suggests that the majority of market participants are building long positions and leveraging their collateral (see section 2.3.3). If the deposit and borrow APY are compared, it can be seen that a high utilization rate is the main driver for high interest rates, also with regard to R_{slope1} and R_{slope2} from table 2.1, which are significantly higher for assets than for stablecoins.

Table 2.2 Top 10 assets on AAVE by total supply. (Own representation)[8]

Asset	Total supply	Total borrowed	Total liquidity	U	$U_{optimal}$	Spread ($U_{optimal}$-U)	Deposit APY	Borrow APY
USDC	3,585.95	3,214.95	371.00	89.65%	90.00%	0.35%	3.42%	4.07%
DAI	1,958.17	1,559.00	399.16	79.62%	80.00%	0.38%	2.93%	4.05%
USDT	1,121.83	990.67	131.16	88.31%	90.00%	1.69%	3.28%	4.00%
TUSD	156.98	117.56	39.41	74.89%	80.00%	5.11%	2.72%	3.82%
ETH	5,921.96	164.90	5,757.06	2.78%	65.00%	62.22%	0.01%	0.34%
WBTC	2,251.44	115.94	2,135.50	5.15%	65.00%	59.85%	0.03%	0.64%
LINK	741.34	5.26	736.08	0.71%	45.00%	44.29%	0.00%	0.11%
MKR	156.50	2.28	154.22	1.45%	45.00%	43.55%	0.00%	0.23%
XSUSHI	125.62	0.25	125.37	0.20%	45.00%	44.80%	0.00%	0.03%
YFI	97.79	29.79	68.00	30.46%	45.00%	14.54%	1.16%	4.85%

Numbers in millions of USD

[7] Wrapped Bitcoin (WBTC) is an ERC-20 token backed 1:1 with Bitcoin (see section 2.1.3).
[8] Status 11/11/2021.

3 Liquidations

If collateral is deposited with an LP and used to take out a loan, this exposes the borrower to liquidation risk. This risk increases steadily as the loan approaches the LTV and the associated liquidation threshold, which represents the minimum acceptable collateral-to-credit ratio. When LT is reached, the borrower defaults, which means that his collateral is liquidated to cover the loan amount due.

The only reason why a liquidation is carried out is because the health factor of a borrow position drops below 1 (see equation 1). The drivers for this can vary, but in the end it is paramount that $\sum(Collateral \times LT) < \sum(Borrowed + Fees)$ so that the collateral becomes eligible for liquidation.

This happens when the asset used as collateral falls in price while the loan remains stable or falls less sharply. This scenario is especially important for a long strategy, where the user deposits his assets as collateral to get stablecoins (see section 2.3.3). If expectations are not met and the market turns bearish, or a sudden event causes the price of the collateral to fall sharply, there is a risk of liquidation.

Vice versa, this applies if the value of the borrowed amount increases while the collateral does not, or not strongly enough, increase in value.

The fact that not only crypto assets are affected by this price change risk is shown by a case from November 2020, when Compound liquidated more than $100 million in value. An error with an external oracle that provides the price of the dollar pegged stablecoin DAI for the Compound network caused DAI to be listed for $1.3 for a short period of time, resulting in borrowed DAI holdings

---

Supplementary Information The online version contains supplementary material available at https://doi.org/10.1007/978-3-658-39056-3_3.

M. Schaible, *Decentralized Lending*, BestMasters,
https://doi.org/10.1007/978-3-658-39056-3_3

from users also seeing a 30% increase in value (Gogo 2020). As a result, many loans were undercollateralized and thus eligible for liquidation.

If a position is undercollateralized, the two dominant liquidation mechanisms are a non-atomic auction and an atomic fixed spread strategy (Qin et al 2021a). Atomic transactions follow the same logic as already explained for Flash Loans, all changes take place during one transaction (see section 2.2; Bartoletti et al. 2020). If it is not completed or an error occurs, no state change takes place. In the event of liquidation, the borrowed item remains in the possession of the user, while the deposited collateral is realized (Perez et al. 2021).

The first concept, a liquidation by auction, is applied by MakerDAO and follows the mechanism of an English auction. In an English or open ascending auction, additional information is available to participants, such as the number of bidders, their bids, and the prices at which they dropped out (Krishna 2010).

A liquidator starts the auction process as soon as $H_f < 1$ is reached for a loan. Interested liquidators then submit their bids for the collateral, whereby this process can take several hours. The auction ends when the framework rules defined for this purpose have been reached and the highest bidder receives the collateral (MakerDAO 2021). A special characteristic of MakerDAO is the distinction between a tend and dent phase of the auction. While the liquidators compete in the tendency phase by making an offer to repay parts of the debt in exchange for all of the collateral, where each new bid must outbid the previous one, a switch is made to the dent phase once the value of the bids d_i reach the value of the loan D ($d_i = D$).

In the dent phase, liquidators compete by submitting bids to accept diminishing collateral c_i in exchange for the full debt that they will eventually repay. Thus, at the end of the auction, the winner repays the full loan and receives a portion of collateral c_{iwin} in return, with the remaining collateral returning to the borrower ($C - c_{iwin}$).

In an atomic fixed spread liquidation, on the other hand, the entire process of liquidation can be handled by only one liquidator. In this form, which is used by Compound and AAVE, a liquidable loan will be liquidated within a transaction, using a flash loan (Qin et al. 2021b) at a predetermined discount. This has the advantage that liquidators do not have to deposit their funds in hour-long auctions and can calculate in advance how much they will earn on a liquidation, since the discount, or liquidation bonus, is already known in advance for the respective asset. In the case of Compound (Leshner and Hayes 2019), this liquidation bonus is determined for all assets in the same way, whereas in the case of AAVE (2021b) it is determined individually for each asset.

3.1 Literature Review

Liquidation is not a new invention of DeFi, as it has been an essential part of finance for decades and has been discussed and researched in terms of liquidation costs (Alderson and Betker 1995), tradeoff between volatility risk and liquidation costs (Almgren and Chriss 1999), liquidation of debt (Reinhart and Shrancia 2011), value-maximizing liquidation policy (Titman 1984) or determinants of the liquidation value of assets (Shleifer and Vishny 1992).

Gudgeon et al. (2020b), Bartoletti et al. (2020), Tolmach et al. (2021) and Kao et al. (2020) investigate the mechanisms, characteristics, and interest rate models of DeFi lending protocols. Gudgeon et al. were the first to refer to protocols that form credit markets based on distributed ledger technology (DLT) as Protocols for Loanable Funds (PLFs). The structure of the interest rate mechanism, as well as its movements and market efficiency, has been empirically studied by them. Bartoletti et al., Perez et al. and Tolmach et al. used this as a basis for their studies and developed models for lending pools by using formal process algebraic techniques to model DeFi protocols, thereby introducing synergies with other DeFi protocols. Kao et al. gave an overview of market risks and liquidation mechanism, after which they performed agent-based modeling and simulation-based stress test on the Compound protocol, with the result that the protocol is able to scale a larger market and offers only a small probability of default despite volatile conditions. To simulate the interactions between liquidations in lending pools and exchanges during periods of high price volatility, Gudgeon et al. (2020a) developed a liquidation model.

Already in 2019, Alethio analyzed the risks associated with Decentralized Lending, focusing on illiquidity in the wake of bank runs. The result underlines the centrality problem of the early DeFi protocols, as in 5 cases a single transaction was enough to drain a quarter of the available pool liquidity. An important role in terms of the first in-depth empirical analysis of liquidations on protocols for loanable funds is played by Darlin et al. (2020), who studied liquidation auctions on MakerDAO, as well as Kao et al. (2020) and ZenGo (2019), who analyzed the liquidation mechanisms on Compound. Frangella (2020) studied the impact of black Thursday, when crypto assets suffered a massive price drop within 24 hours and finds that the liquidation rate on AAVE was 100 times higher than the average amount liquidated. In doing so, they compare liquidation mechanisms and develop a methodology to do this according to objective standards, also taking into account the risks of market participants.

3.2 Empirical Evidence and Method

As the literature review shows, there are already a few empirical analyses on the topic of liquidations in Decentralized Lending pools, but these are mainly concerned with the underlying mechanism, general risks, or profitability of liquidations. However, there is still no relevant analysis of the extent to which price fluctuations of the underlying correlate with liquidations. Furthermore, it is unclear whether high price losses trigger most liquidations or whether liquidations also take place when the price development of the deposited collateral is positive.

In order to obtain information about the dependency structure of the two characteristics liquidations and returns, a scatter plot is used in the first step. The graphical representation of the static characteristics of the two pairs of values results in a recognizable pattern, whereby initial correlations can already be detected visually. The regression line generated in this scatter plot, a fixed line formed from the available data, shows the overall trend of the dataset, again allowing a relationship to be mapped between the two variables.

For a statistical measurement of the relationship between liquidations and returns as well as the quantifiability of the linear correlation, a regression analysis is performed. For this purpose, the ordinary least squares (OLS) method was chosen as it can be well applied for a single explanatory variable. In this case, liquidations form the dependent variable and returns serve as the independent variable or regressor.

Subsequently, the relationship between negative returns and high liquidations is examined using the two-means test, for which the means of the returns of the 30 highest and lowest liquidations are used.

A two-proportions test is also performed, in which the relative number of liquidations in two different samples is compared. This type of hypothesis testing is used to find out whether the results of a test are valid or repeatable.

3.3 Data Description

The data examined is on-chain data from AAVE V2 and covers the period from 01 January 2021 to 09 June 2021. In order to crawl the data from the blockchain, the following procedure was applied.

The first step is to find the AAVE lending pool V2 contract address, which can be accessed by typing in Etherscan.io "Aave: Lending Pool V2" and is "*0×7d2768dE32b0b80b7a3454c06BdAc94A69DDc7A9*". For this contract address the desired topic hash must be found, which describes the different utilities in the LP and defines events like deposit, borrow or liquidation depending on the selection. This topic hash can be generated via the Covalent topic generator (Covalent 2021b) by entering the contract address of the LP and results in the following hash for the liquidation call "*0xe413a321e8681d831f4dbccbca790d2952b56f977908e45be37335533e005286*". In order to pull the data for the liquidation call events for the AAVE lending pool V2 from the blockchain, an account at Covalent API (2021a) is required, which provides the key with which API requests can be authenticated. API stands for Application Programming Interface, which is an interface that can be used to communicate with blockchain nodes (Scheid et al. 2019). The following command is now entered via REQBIN (REQBIN 2021) to convert the requested liquidation call event from blockchain data into a JSON format:

curl -X GET https://api.covalenthq.com/v1/1/events/topics/0xe413a321e8681d831f4dbccbca790d2952b56f977908e45be37335533e005286/?starting-block=11569878&ending-block=12601121&senderaddress=0x7d2768dE32b0b80b7a3454c06BdAc94A69DDc7A9&page-size=9999&key=ckey_880ae046a62440168d4d15d0f30 \ -H "Accept: application/json"

where "*1*" is the chain ID, in this case Ethereum, and "*0xe413a321e8681d831f4dbccbca790d2952b56f977908e45be37335533e005286*" is the topic hash, here liquidations call events. As already explained in section 2.1.1, a blockchain is composed of chronological blocks, which explains why a certain block must be specified as the start and end point of the search. The sender address in this case is again the contract address of the AAVE lending pool V2. The key used is the one created in the Covalent API account and authenticates the whole query. Depending on the requirements, the topic hash can also be changed with this command to retrieve information on the events deposit, borrow, withdraws or flash loans, for example.

If the command is executed and the data is output in JSON format, it can be simply copied and converted to a csv file via sites like convertcsv.com (convertcsv.com 2021).

For the analysis, the five assets that were most frequently deposited as collateral in liquidations during the period under review were selected. These are wrapped Ether (WETH), wrapped Bitcoin (WBTC), Chainlink (LINK), AAVE and Uniswap (UNI). In addition, the five assets that were most frequently selected as debt assets in liquidations were examined. The currencies in this case are USDC, DAI, Binance USD (BUSD), Gemini Dollar (GUSD) and Tether (USDT).

Moreover, the daily opening prices of these ten assets were taken from the Coinmarketcap website.

Unlike stock prices, there is no need to adjust (Sauer 1991) for splits, dividends or subscription rights, as these do not exist, and there is also no need to adjust for weekends or holidays, as crypto exchanges are open around the clock.

The period which will be studied in more detail is from May 15 to May 25, as this is the period during which over 75% of all observed liquidations occurred. The hourly opening prices examined here were obtained from the Binance Exchange Data website.

3.4 Analysis

In order to identify the extent to which liquidations are influenced by the price of the underlying, it is worthwhile to first obtain an overview of the liquidations in the period under review.

In the period from 01 January 2021 to 09 June 2021, the ten selected assets on the AAVE lending pool V2 saw liquidations totaling $473 million, with over 75% coming from WETH (53.94%) and WBTC (22.3%) alone (attachment 2). It is also worth mentioning that BUSD, GUSD and USDT were not deposited as collateral in any liquidation event during the said period. This supports the observation from table 2.2 and the results of Saengchote (2021), namely that assets such as WETH and WBTC are preferably used as collateral, whereas stablecoins are predominantly borrowed.

To show the distribution over time, the liquidations from the dataset were sorted by day and the corresponding collateral, and the amount was offset against the daily opening price. Figure 3.1 shows the result of this, whereby it is noticeable that in the case of larger liquidation events, all the assets examined were mostly affected. Out of the $473 million liquidations, only $108 million took place from 01 January to May 15, whereas $357 million was liquidated from May 15 to May 25. This uneven distribution is illustrated by the fact that four of the five days with the most liquidations fall within this period, and of these, nearly $200 million collateral was liquidated on May 19 alone, representing 42.18% of the total.

Looking at the daily returns shown in figure 3.2 for the period under consideration, it can already be seen that the returns also reach their lowest value in the period with the most liquidations from figure 6. The lowest day-to-day return was measured from May 19 to May 20 with -36.02% and the highest return from May 24 to May 25 with + 25.76%, which underlines the particularly high volatility

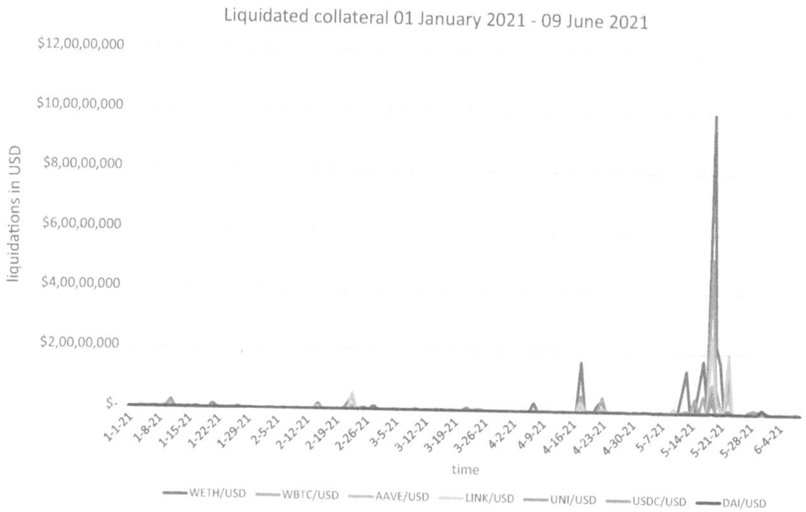

Figure 3.1 Liquidated collateral 01 January 2021–09 June 2021. (Own representation)

in this narrow time window. The daily mean is 0.62%, which means that the five examined assets have developed positively over the period. This is even 3.01% if the return of Bitcoin is excluded, which recorded the lowest value increase with 15.25% (see attachment 3).[1]

In order to examine the impact of price fluctuations of the underlying securities on liquidations, the period from May 15 to May 25 is examined in more detail, as this was the period in which most liquidations took place, and it also has the highest price volatility.

Figure 3.3 compares the total liquidations with the average return of the five assets examined in the period 15–25 May on an hourly basis (GMT + 0). As can be seen in figures 3.1 and 3.2, May 19 was the day with the highest number of liquidations and the highest hourly price loss. It is striking that after the price slide at 1 pm (−20.54%), liquidations amounting to just under $53 million took place at 2 pm. A conclusion could be drawn from this figure that high liquidations follow high price losses by looking at the returns on May 19 at 1 pm, May 20 at 0 am, May 21 at 3 pm or May 23 at 9 am and 1 pm.

[1] Value increase: WETH 240.27%, WBTC 15.25%, AAVE 276.98%, LINK 113.93%, UNI 353.38%.

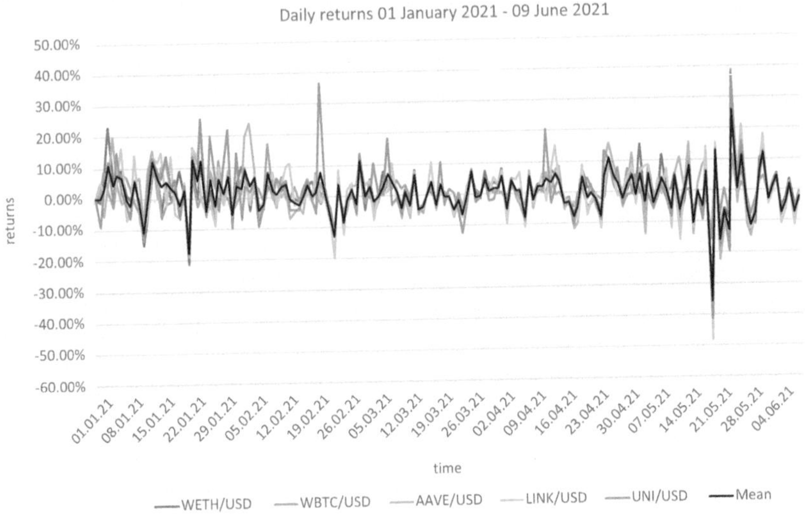

Figure 3.2 Daily returns 01 January 2021–09 June 2021. (Own representation)

Looking at the five assets in detail, all have their highest liquidations on May 19 between 12 and 2 p.m., so it can be said that the amounts in figure 3.3 do not result from an overweighting of a particular asset at that time (see attachment 4).

To examine the observation that high liquidations are followed by high price declines, in the subsequent section the return in the corresponding hour of liquidation is considered on the one hand and one hour before liquidation on the other hand.

Figure 3.4 serves as a first overview of the distribution of liquidations in relation to their underlying return. This scatter plot shows the liquidations of the five assets studied during the period from May 15 to May 25, with each point summarizing the liquidations for one hour. The return prevailing in those hours is determined from the average of the five sample returns for the relevant period. For clarity, the liquidation amounts on the x-axis are shown with a logarithm of 100. It can be seen that most of the liquidations per hour are in the mid four-digit range, which is underlined by a median of \$32,462, and also the corresponding returns are in the range from −5% to + 5% but tend to be rather negative as a median of −0.3402% illustrates. Overall, there is quite a widespread along the regression line, especially the liquidations in the double-digit million range deviate significantly, with an amount of \$19.32 million being the exception. A

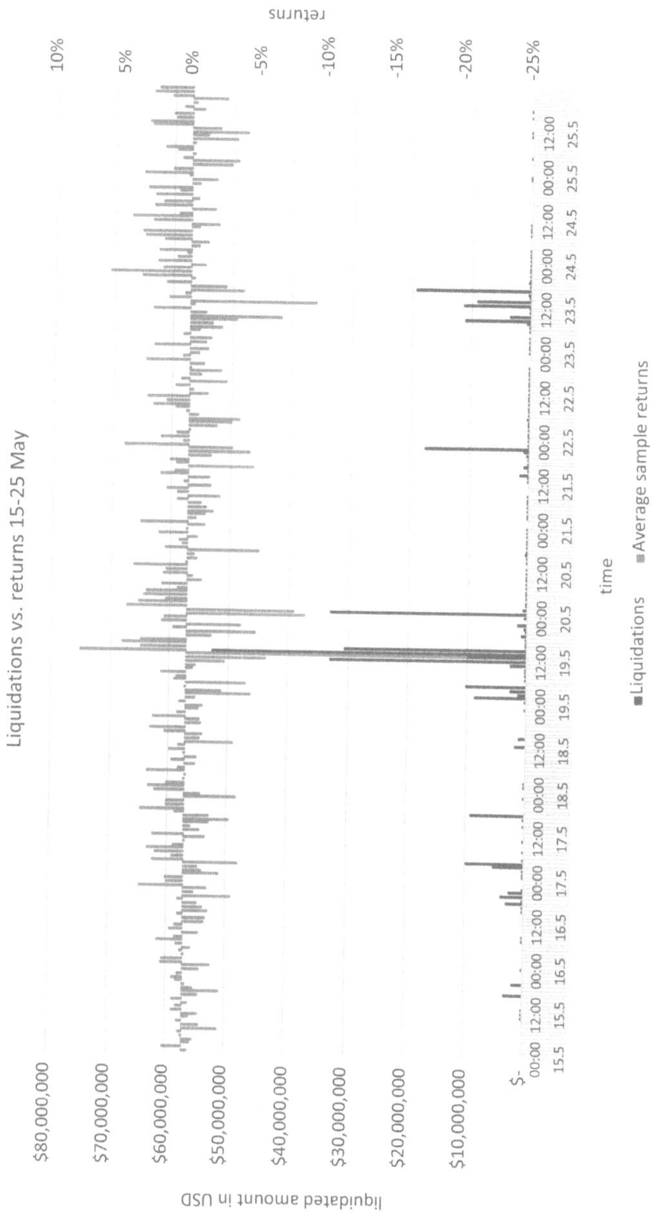

Figure 3.3 Liquidations vs. returns 15–25 May. (Own representation)

similar allocation can also be seen in the scatter plots if the assets are considered individually and with their own return. For example, AAVE, LINK and UNI also suffered their highest liquidations at a time when the return for that hour was in quite a high positive range (see attachment 5).

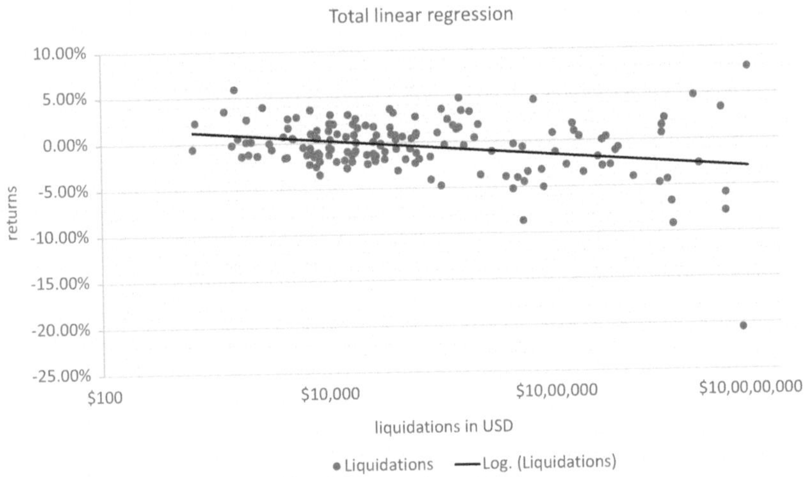

Figure 3.4 Distribution of liquidations according to returns. (Own representation)

If these observations are compared with figure 3.5, which shows the liquidations with the returns that occurred one hour earlier, it is evident that the liquidations are now positioned much more closely around the regression line. Especially the liquidations larger than $300,000 are now oriented much closer to the regression line and no longer show such high positive returns. The outlier is a liquidation of $30.52 million with a return of 7.80% and the largest liquidation of $52.62 million with a return of −20.54%. The same shift can be observed when looking at the five individual assets, where the highest liquidations are always associated with a negative return (see attachment 6). At first glance, it can be observed that the returns one hour before are more decisive for the liquidations than the yields at the time of liquidation, which is reflected by the tighter arrangement around the regression line as well as the smaller (positive) outliers.

In addition, a shift towards more negative returns can be observed. This is underlined by the median of the one hour earlier returns, which is −0.4369% and the skewness, which is −1.9715 and was −1.8616 for the returns in figure 3.4 (see attachment 7).

If the distributions of liquidation-triggering returns at the time of liquidation and one hour before are compared (see attachment 8), it is also apparent that there is a slight shift to the left in the direction of negative returns. However, this shift takes place exclusively in the range from −5% to + 5%; the tails of the distribution are not affected.

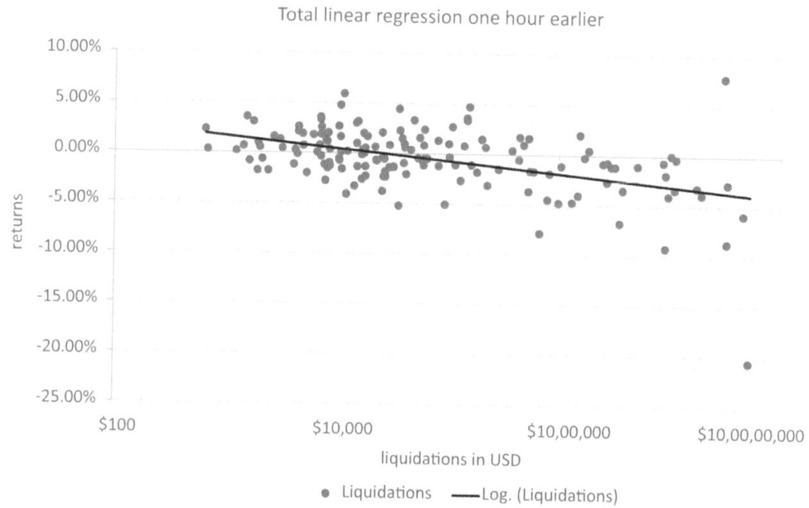

Figure 3.5 Distribution of liquidations according to returns one hour earlier. (Own representation)

If the liquidations in USD from figures 3.4 and 3.5 are ranked, a classic Pareto distribution can be seen. In the case of liquidations, the "80–20 rule" is even tightened, as in this scenario 10.32% of the hourly liquidations are responsible for 89.01% of the liquidated USD amount (see attachment 9). It is noteworthy that the hourly returns of these 10.32% liquidations are 62.50% negative and the returns one hour before are even 87.50% negative.[2]

For a statistical measurement of the relationship between liquidations and returns, a regression analysis is carried out. For this purpose, the Ordinary Least

[2] The returns for all liquidations in this period are negative only in 53.55% (83/155) of the cases. If the returns are taken one hour earlier, they are 54.84% (85/155).

Squares (OLS) method was chosen, as it can be applied well for a single explanatory variable. In this case, liquidations form the dependent variable and returns serve as the independent variable or regressor.

Therefore, OLS regressions were ran on the one hand for the cumulative sample data and on the other hand for the five assets to be examined individually.

Table 3.1 gives an overview of the OLS results. The regression was performed with the liquidations per hour as the dependent variable and the returns generated in these hours as the independent variable. Since all liquidations that occurred during a full hour are aggregated, the number of observations indicates in how many of the 264 hours between May 15 and May 25 2021 liquidations occurred.

Looking at the results of the OLS, it is noticeable that the coefficient of AAVE and UNI is positive, while the others have a high negative value.

The sign of a regression coefficient indicates whether there is a positive or negative correlation between the individual independent variables and the dependent variable. Accordingly, a positive coefficient indicates that the mean value of the dependent variable tends to increase when the value of the independent variable increases, whereas a negative coefficient indicates that the dependent variable tends to decrease when the value of the independent variable increases. A negative value is therefore what could be expected here, since with a positive increasing return the number of liquidations would decrease, which in turn would lower the mean of liquidations.

The positive correlation of liquidations to returns can also be seen in the T-ratio for AAVE and UNI. Furthermore, the T-ratio indicates that returns had a significant impact on the output of liquidations for LINK and the entire sample data, and the smallest impact for AAVE and UNI.

Assuming a significance level of 5%, it can be said with a 95% probability that the independent variable, in this case the return, has some effect on the dependent variable if the P-value is 5% or less. In this case, AAVE and UNI must again be mentioned, whose P-values of 54.16% and 11.39%, respectively, are well above the 5% threshold. The impact of the immediate negative returns on liquidations is therefore statistically significant in only four out of six samples. In addition, it should be mentioned that the value of WETH, at 4.9%, is also only minimally below the significance level.

As with the T-ratio, the results of R-squared again highlight LINK and the sample data with the highest values and, consequently, the highest proportion of variation in their dependent variables explained by their independent variables. Since in a regression with a single independent variable it is the same as the square of the correlation between the dependent and the independent variable, these two data sets also have the highest correlation between liquidations and returns. A negative adjusted R-squared value in AAVE shows no correlation of the variables and can be read as zero.

The results of the OLS test indicate that the returns, occurred at the time of liquidation, cannot adequately explain the liquidations, since only four of six samples are negatively correlated and also have a significant P-value. Furthermore, the fact that the highest R-squared is only 10.27% supports this argument.

Table 3.1 OLS summary output. (Own representation)

	Sample	WETH	WBTC	AAVE	LINK	UNI
Observations	155	135	88	55	112	57
Mean	2,247,893	1,389,121	969,698	311,702	461,728	117,567
Coefficient	− 65,034,523	− 22,497,711	− 34,078,490	1,960,461	− 10,664,451	1,702,880
Std. error	18,734,641	11,322,285	13,147,208	3,191,170	3,004,918	1,060,099
T-ratio	− 3.4714	− 1.9870	− 2.5921	0.6143	− 3.5490	1.6063
P-value	0.0007	0.0490	0.0112	0.5416	0.0006	0.1139
R-squared	0.0730	0.0288	0.0725	0.0071	0.1027	0.0448
Adj. R-squared	0.0670	0.0215	0.0617	− 0.0117	0.0946	0.0274

The OLS method was also performed with the returns one hour before liquidation as the independent variable, with the liquidations again forming the dependent variable.

The results are given in table 3.2 and already show clear differences in the coefficients compared with the figures in table 3.1. Thus, AAVE and UNI now also have a strongly negative coefficient, and those of the other datasets have again decreased significantly. The exception is WBTC, with a coefficient decrease of only about 13.26%.

All data sets now have a negative correlation between the dependent and independent variable, as seen by the negative coefficients and the negative T-ratio.

In the case of the P-values, there are no outliers in these OLS results as in table 3; all data sets have very low values in this case. Once again, assuming a significance level of 5%, it can be said that the return one hour before liquidation has an impact on the dependent variable (liquidations).

UNI and AAVE have the highest R-squared values, explaining 41.06% and 28.76% of their dependent variables by the independent variable, respectively. The R-squared values of the other datasets have also risen to double-digit percentages, with only WBTC remaining below the 10% threshold at 8.53%.

The negative correlation of all data sets supports the hypothesis that negative returns on collateral are a major reason for liquidations. The consistently low

P-values and significantly higher R-squared values also suggest that the returns one hour before the liquidations have a greater influence on these and are more suitable as a measure. The fact that a maximum of 41.06% (UNI) of the liquidations can be explained by the returns suggests that the returns have not yet been selected precisely enough. One of the main reasons for this is that only the opening prices of the respective hour were taken into account, which shows and gives an idea of the influence, but does not reflect the exact returns that could ultimately have caused the liquidation. In addition, the liquidation may also have been triggered by an increase in the price of the borrowed value (see chapter 3), even if the vast majority of the loans are made in stablecoins (Saengchote 2021).

Table 3.2 OLS summary output returns one hour earlier. (Own representation)

	Sample	WETH	WBTC	AAVE	LINK	UNI
Observations	155	135	88	55	112	57
Mean	2,247,893	1,389,121	969,698	311,702	461,728	117,567
Coefficient	– 118,928,342	– 55,407,420	– 38,596,899	– 9,748,155	– 17,545,718	– 5,681,086
Std. error	17,288,946	10,960,237	13,629,481	2,107,459	2,758,625	917,884
T-ratio	– 6.8789	– 5.0553	– 2.8319	– 4.6255	– 6.3603	– 6.1893
P-value	1.45E-10	1.39E-06	0.0058	2.44E-05	4.73E-09	7.94E-08
R-squared	0.2362	0.1612	0.0853	0.2876	0.2689	0.4106
Adj. R-squared	0.2312	0.1549	0.0747	0.2742	0.2622	0.3998

To illustrate the relationship between negative returns and high liquidations, a two -means test was carried out. For this purpose, the 30 highest and lowest hourly liquidations in the period from May 15 to May 25 were considered.[3] The results of this test, which was carried out on the one hand with the returns at the time of liquidation and on the other hand with the returns one hour earlier, are shown in table 3.3.

The null hypothesis for these two-means tests is:

$$H_0 : \mu_1 = \mu_2$$

This states that the mean of the returns is the same for the 30 highest and lowest hourly liquidations. The alternative hypothesis is that the means are not equal. This is written as:

$$H_1 : \mu_1 \neq \mu_2$$

[3] Note: Lowest liquidation = $0 liquidation, as there are 109 of these in the sample, those closest in time to the highest 30 liquidations were selected.

When comparing the means, it can be seen that the 30 highest liquidations are negative for the means of the associated returns, while the 30 lowest have slightly positive means. Also, the standard distribution is significantly higher for the two Max samples than for the Min, which is due to the fact that the range of returns is from −20.54% to 7.80%.

Consequently, the null hypothesis that the means are equal can be rejected and it can be stated that the hourly means of the Max and Min samples differ significantly from each other and even diverge further if the returns are considered one hour earlier. This is supported by the test statistics of $t_{returns}(58) = -2.9024$ and $t_{returns-1}(58) = -3.5636$, which show a significant difference between the returns of the 30 maximum and 30 minimum liquidations. With respect to the P-value, it can be said that both two-means tests show statistical relevance, again assuming a significance level of 5%. Thus, it could be confirmed that negative returns are associated with high liquidations, whereas no liquidations can also have negative returns in individual cases but have a positive mean in total and the standard deviation is also significantly lower.

Table 3.3 Two means test returns and returns one hour earlier. (Own representation)

	Returns		**Returns one hour earlier**	
Sample	Max	Min	Max	Min
N	30	30	30	30
Mean	– 0.0209	0.0072	– 0.0294	0.0033
Std. Dev.	0.0510	0.0143	0.0462	0.0120
Std. error of mean	0.0093	0.0026	0.0084	0.0036
Test statistics: t(58)	– 2.9024		– 3.5636	
Two-tailed P-value	0.0052		0.0007	

In addition, the period under review was compared with the period of the same length within the sample from January to June 2021, during which the fewest liquidations occurred. The corresponding period is from March 27 to April 6, 2021. For this purpose, a two-proportions test was applied, in which the respective proportions of liquidations are compared with each other.

The null hypothesis for these two-proportions tests is:

$$H_0 : p_1 = p_2$$

This states that the sample proportion is the same for the time periods in March and May. The alternative hypothesis is that the sample proportion is not equal. This is written as:

$$H_1 : p_1 \neq p_2$$

Table 3.4 shows the results, whereby the decisive factor is in how many of the 264 hours per period liquidations have occurred. It can be seen that the hourly mean for the period is slightly positive in March, whereas it is negative in May. More serious are the differences in standard deviation and volatility, both of which are significantly higher in May than in March. Since, as mentioned, the period with the most liquidations is compared with the period with the least, it is not surprising that there were liquidations in only 5 of the 264 hours of the March period, whereas in May there were liquidations in 58.71%, or 155/264, of the hours.

The null hypothesis that the sample fraction is the same in March and May can be rejected in this case. The value of z is 14.2044, which in conjunction with a P-value of 8.598e-46 at a significance level of 5% indicates that the result of the two-proportions test is statistically significant. In this case, the many liquidations in the May period are again accompanied by a negative hourly mean and a high volatility, whereas the mean in March is slightly positive and the volatility five times lower.

Table 3.4
Two-proportions test. (Own representation)

	March	May
N	264	264
Mean (returns)	0.0005	− 0.0012
Std. Dev. (returns)	0.0050	0.0266
Volatility (returns)	0.0811	0.4323
Liquidations occurred	5	155
Proportions (liquidations)	0.0189	0.5871
Test statistics (z)	14.2044	
Two-tailed P-value	8.598e-46	

4 Conclusion

In a first step, this paper has aimed to provide an overview of the functioning of decentralized loans, including a closer look at the composition of interest rates, especially regarding the influence of supply and demand. Furthermore, the extent to which fluctuations in the price of the collateral deposited had an impact on its liquidation was determined.

In order to understand the concept of lending on the blockchain, the basic principles of blockchain technology were briefly presented. The importance of smart contracts for DeFi was highlighted, whereby the elements of autonomy, self-sufficiency and decentralization can be named here as representative of the mechanism. To illustrate the interaction of blockchain and smart contracts, the DeFi architecture was explained using the so-called Schär model. In this multi-layered architecture, each hierarchy has its own specific role, with particular importance given to the settlement layer, which contains the underlying blockchain. The leading role of Ethereum should be emphasized here, on which 73% of the DeFi market capitalization is built.

The final instance of this architecture is the application layer, on which dApps can be built, and to which the lending pool platforms examined here also belong. Both supplying and borrowing on these platforms is done via a pool-based strategy, whereby the lender adds funds to a lending pool and the borrower takes loans from it. The characteristic here is that lending is done via overcollateralized loans, so that funds must first be added to an LP in order to be entitled to lend them up to a certain LTV. The interest that creditors receive, and debtors must pay is derived from the supply and demand for the respective LP. The utilization rate describes the ratio of total borrows to total supplies, where $U = 1$ denotes a situation in which there is no more free liquidity available. While this status leads to quite high interest rates in order to be attractive to potential lenders and unattractive to potential borrowers on the one hand, it also creates a liquidity

M. Schaible, *Decentralized Lending*, BestMasters,
https://doi.org/10.1007/978-3-658-39056-3_4

risk on the other. This liquidity risk manifests itself in the fact that not all orders can be fulfilled if more funds are to be withdrawn from the LP than it has available in liquidity, which represents a significant risk for users, especially in the event of a bank run. For this reason, the most commonly used interest rate model on lending platforms is the so-called kinked rates model, which sharply changes the rate as soon as the point of optimal utilization rate $U_{optimal}$. is exceeded. Consequently, LPs using a non-linear interest rate model would have to have a significantly higher liquidity volume than LPs with kinked interest rates to compete with their interest rates while averting $U = 1$. Linear rate models do not have this problem, but do not provide any built-in protection to react to a too high utilization rate.

In order to answer the question of the influence of price fluctuations of the collateral deposited on its liquidation, a comprehensive data set on on-chain data from AAVE V2 was created, the content of which is analyzed using quantitative methods and the conclusions drawn are described. In the studied period from 01 January 2021 to 09 June 2021, collateral in the amount of $473 million was liquidated, of which WETH and WBTC accounted for over 75%. It is striking that the share of liquidated stablecoins deposited as collateral accounts for <3.5% of this sum. It can be concluded that the majority of collaterals during this period consisted of crypto assets that users deposited in order to benefit from the high interest rates on them and to participate in the price gains at the same time. This implies a bullish market view, especially considering that most positions have experienced even higher exposure through the use of leverage.

Looking at the period from 15 May 2021 to 25 May 2021, in which 75.48% of the total liquidations took place, it is striking that a correlation to high negative returns can already be observed when comparing hourly liquidations and returns of the collaterals. Subsequently, this period was examined using the hourly opening prices at the hour of liquidation and one hour in advance. One insight that can be drawn from the scatter plots is that the returns one hour earlier describe the liquidations more decisively, since the results are tighter around the regression line and there are fewer outliers. In addition, a shift towards more negative returns in the case of means and skewness can be observed. These findings are supported by the OLS, which did not yet provide any meaningful data with the returns at the time of liquidation but did with the returns one hour earlier. The negative correlation of all data sets supports the hypothesis that negative returns on collateral are a major reason for liquidations. The consistently low P-values and significantly higher R-squared values also suggest that returns one hour before liquidations have a greater impact on them and are more suitable as a measure.

The findings that negative returns are associated with high liquidations were confirmed with a two-means test, in which both the T-values and P-values were once again statistically more significant for the returns one hour earlier than for the returns at the hour of liquidation. The period under review was also compared with the period in which the fewest liquidations took place using a two-proportions test. Again, it was confirmed that the numerous liquidations in May are accompanied by a negative hourly mean and high volatility in terms of returns, while the mean in the period with the fewest liquidations is slightly positive and volatility is five times lower.

In summary, it can be said that price fluctuations of collaterals are closely related to their liquidations, especially high negative rewards and high liquidations are strongly correlated. In addition, it was found that returns one hour before liquidations are a better measure than those at the time of liquidation, which is due to the fact that liquidations are a reaction to undercollateralization and liquidators within the network have to address it first. In addition, it was found that liquidations also took place although the returns at the time of liquidation as well as one hour before were positive. In this case, it is obvious that the liquidation was caused by an increase in the value of the borrowed asset or that the measurement was incorrect. Furthermore, based on the results of this work, it should be easier to obtain data in the future and the data set could be expanded. The fact that more and more research papers and studies are dealing with the topic of Decentralized Finance, which leads to a higher data density and comparability, also contributes to this.

This introduces the limitations of this thesis. While the results show the influence of the returns, the fact that only the opening prices of the respective hours were taken precludes a more precise analysis of which returns were ultimately responsible for the liquidation. This leads to distortions, as undercollateralization can result from price fluctuations that occurred within a minute but were eliminated in the hour-to-hour analysis. Likewise, only the price fluctuations of the collaterals deposited were examined; again, a comparison with the corresponding borrowed assets and their price development should be carried out in future research.

The influence of leverage can also only be inadequately explained in this thesis; here, too, it would be useful to work with minute-by-minute data and to examine the number of leveraged wallets and their volume at major liquidation events in more detail.

The composition of interest rates should also be examined to determine whether they correlate with liquidations and to what extent price fluctuations affect the utilization rate as well as inflows and outflows of lending pools. This would help to better understand liquidation events and derive patterns, which in turn would allow the establishment of early warning systems that can be integrated into portfolio management tools.

Literature

AAVE (2020): 'Protocol Whitepaper V1.0'. URL: https://academy.bit2me.com/wp-content/uploads/2021/07/Aave_Protocol_Whitepaper_v1_0.pdf [Accessed 22.10.2021].

AAVE (2021a): 'Borrow Interest Rate'. URL: https://docs.aave.com/risk/liquidity-risk/borrow-interest-rate [Accessed 09.11.2021a].

AAVE (2021b): 'Risk Parameters'. URL: https://docs.aave.com/risk/asset-risk/risk-parameters [Accessed 15.11.2021b].

AAVE (2022): 'Overview USDC'. URL: https://app.aave.com/reserve-overview/USDC-0xa0b86991c6218b36c1d19d4a2e9eb0ce3606eb480xb53c1a33016b2dc2ff3653530bff1848a515c8c5 [Accessed 09.02.2022].

Aavewatch (2021): 'Total Aave stats'. URL: https://v2.aavewatch.com [Accessed 10.11.2021].

Abadi, J., Brunnermeier, M. (2018): 'Blockchain Economics'. Working paper 25407, National Bureau of Economic Research, Cambridge.

Alderson, M., Betker, B. (1995): 'Liquidation costs and capital structure'. In: Journal of Financial Economics 39, 1, pp. 45–69.

Alethio (2019): 'Illiquidity and Bank Run Risk in Defi'. URL: https://medium.com/alethio/overlooked-risk-illiquidity-and-bank-runs-on-compound-finance-5d6fc3922d0d [Accessed 19.11.2021].

Alharby, M., van Moorsel, A. (2017): 'Blockchain-based Smart Contracts: A Systematic Mapping Study'. Fourth International Conference on Computer Science and Information Technology (CSIT-2017), pp. 125–140.

Almgrenand, R., Chriss, N. (1999): 'Value under liquidation'. In: Risk12, 12, pp. 61–63.

Amler, H., Eckey L., Faust, S., Kaiser, M., Sandner, P., Schlosser, B. (2021): 'DeFi-ning DeFi: Challenges & Pathway'. URL: arXiv:2101.05589 [Accessed 21.10.2021].

Anchor Protocol (2022): 'Earn'. URL: https://app.anchorprotocol.com/earn [Accessed 09.02.2022].

Arrunada, B., Garicano L. (2018): 'Blockchain: The Birth of Decentralized Governance'. Working paper 1038, GSE Working Paper Series, Barcelona.

Bartoletti, M., Chiang, J., Lafuente, A. (2020): SoK: 'Lending Pools in Decentralized Finance'. In: Bernhard M. et al. (eds) 'Financial Cryptography and Data Security. FC

M. Schaible, *Decentralized Lending*, BestMasters,
https://doi.org/10.1007/978-3-658-39056-3

2021 International Workshops'. FC 2021. Lecture Notes in Computer Science, vol 12676. Springer, Berlin, Heidelberg, pp. 553–578.

Bavosa, A. (2020): 'Borrowing Assets from the Compound Protocol'. URL https://medium.com/compound-finance/borrowing-assets-from-compound-quick-start-guide-f5c69af4b8f4 [Accessed 30.10.2021].

builtin.com beta (2021): 'Blockchain'. URL: https://builtin.com/blockchain [Accessed 03.11.2021].

Buterin, V. (2013): 'A Next-Generation Smart Contract and Decentralized Application Platform'. URL: https://ethereum.org/en/whitepaper/ [Accessed 04.09.2021].

Cao, S., Cong L., Baozhong Y. (2018), 'Auditing and Blockchains: Pricing, Misstatements and Regulation'. mimeo, Chicago.

Castro-Iragorri, C., Ramirez, J., Velez, S. (2021): 'Financial intermediation and risk in decentralized lending protocols'. Working paper, Universidad del Rosario, Colombia.

Coingecko (2021): 'Globale Kryptowährungs-Charts: Gesamte Marktkapitalisierung'. URL: https://www.coingecko.com/de/global_charts [Accessed 25.10.2021].

Compound Labs, Inc. (2020): 'DAI rate model'. URL: https://etherscan.io/address/0xfed941d39905b23d6faf02c8301d40bd4834e27f#code [Accessed 09.11.2021].

Convertscv.com (2021): 'Convert JSON to CSV'. URL: https://www.convertcsv.com/json-to-csv.htm [Accessed 25.11.2021].

Cousaert, S., Xu, J., Matsui, T. (2021): 'SoK: Yield Aggregators in DeFi'. URL: https://arxiv.org/pdf/2105.13891.pdf [Accessed 02.11.2021].

Covalent (2021a): 'Join Covalent'. URL: https://www.covalenthq.com/platform/#/auth/register [Accessed 25.11.2021a].

Covalent (2021b): 'Topic Calculator'. URL: https://www.covalenthq.com/docs/tools/topic-calculator [Accessed 25.11.2021b].

Defi-Pulse (2021a): 'Total Value Locked (USD) in DeFi'. URL: https://defipulse.com [Accessed 25.10.2021a].

Defi-Pulse (2021b): 'Total Value Locked (USD) in Lending'. URL: https://defipulse.com [Accessed 25.10.2021b].

Defi-Pulse (2022): 'Total Value Locked (USD) in Lending'. URL: https://defipulse.com [Accessed 13.02.2022].

Delmolino K., Arnett M., Kosba A., Miller A., Shi E. (2016): 'Step by Step Towards Creating a Safe Smart Contract: Lessons and Insights from a Cryptocurrency Lab'. In: Clark J., Meiklejohn S., Ryan P., Wallach D., Brenner M., Rohloff K. (eds), 'Financial Cryptography and Data Security'. FC 2016. Lecture Notes in Computer Science, vol 9604. Springer, Berlin, Heidelberg, pp. 79–94.

dYdX (2019): 'Polynomial Interest Setter'. URL: https://etherscan.io/address/0xaEE83ca85Ad63DFA04993adcd76CB2B3589eCa49#code [Accessed 09.11.2021].

Evans, D. (2014): 'Economic Aspects of Bitcoin and Other Decentralized Public-Ledger Currency Platforms'. University of Chicago Coase-Sandor Institute for Law & Economics Research Paper No. 685.

Ethereum Foundation (2021): 'py-evm Documentation Release 0.5.0-alpha.1'. URL: https://py-evm.readthedocs.io/_/downloads/en/latest/pdf/ [Accessed 01.11.2021].

Etherscan (2021): 'Token Tracker ERC-20'. URL: https://etherscan.io/tokens [Accessed 23.10.2021].

Fairfield, J. (2014): 'Smart contracts, Bitcoin bots, and consumer protection'. 71 Wash Lee L Rev Online 36, pp. 35–50.

Frangella, E. (2020): Aave Borrowing Rates Upgraded. URL: https://medium.com/aave/aave-borrowing-rates-upgraded-f6c8b27973a7 [Accessed 10.11.2021].

Gans, J. (2019): 'The fine prints in smart contracts'. Working Paper 25443. National Bureau of Economic Research, Cambridge.

Grigo, J., Hansen, P., Patz, A., von Wachter, V. (2020): 'Decentralized Finance (DeFi)—A new Fintech Revolution?'. BITKOM (German federal association for information technology, telecommunication and new media), Berlin.

Gogo, J. (2020): '$100 Million Liquidated on Defi Protocol Compound Following Oracle Exploit'. URL: https://news.bitcoin.com/100-million-liquidated-on-defi-protocol-compound-following-oracle-exploit/ [Accessed 13.11.2021].

Gudgeon, L., Perez, D., Harz, D., Gervais, A., Livshits, B. (2020a), 'The Decentralized Financial Crisis: Attacking DeFi'. URL: https://arxiv.org/pdf/2002.08099.pdf [Accessed 01.11.2021].

Gudgeon, L., Werner, S., Perez, D., Knottenbelt, W. (2020b): 'DeFi Protocols for Loanable Funds: Interest Rates, Liquidity and Market Efficiency'. AFT '20: Proceedings of the 2nd ACM Conference on Advances in Financial Technologies, pp. 92–112.

Haber, S., Stornetta, S. (1991): 'How to time-stamp a digital document'. Advances in Cryptology: Proceedings of Crypto '90, Menezes and Vanstone, eds., LNCS 537, Springer (1991), pp. 437–455.

Juliano, A. (2017): 'dYdX: A Standard for Decentralized Margin Trading and Derivatives'. URL: https://whitepaper.dydx.exchange [Accessed 09.11.2021].

Kao, H.T., Chitra, T., Chiang, R., Morrow, J. (2020): 'An Analysis of the Market Risk to Participants in the Compound Protocol'. In: Third International Symposium on Foundations and Applications of Blockchain (FAB '20).

Kiong, L. (2020): 'DEFI Handbook: A Comprehensive Guide to Decentralized Finance'. Independently published.

Krishna, V. (2010): 'Auction Theory'. Academic Press, London.

Kulechov, S. (2021): 'Aave and Flash Loans: Uncollateralized Lending in DeFi'. URL: https://www.gemini.com/cryptopedia/aave-flashloans [Accessed 01.11.2021].

Lau, H., Tse, S. (2021): 'Decentralized Basic Income: Creating Wealth with On-Chain Staking and Fixed-Rate Protocols'. URL: https://arxiv.org/abs/2107.14312 [Accessed 25.10.2021].

Leshner, R., Hayes, G. (2019): 'Compound: The Money Market Protocol'. URL: https://compound.finance/documents/Compound.Whitepaper.pdf [Accessed 22.10.2021].

MakerDAO (2021): 'The Maker Protocol: MakerDAO's Multi-Collateral Dai (MCD) System'. URL: https://makerdao.com/en/whitepaper/#abstract [Accessed 22.10.2021].

Merkle, R. (1979): 'Secrecy, authentication, and public-key systems'. PhD. Thesis, Stanford University.

Miller, M. (1997): 'The Future of Law'. In: Paper delivered at the Extro 3 Conference (August 9. 1997) URL: https://drive.google.com/file/d/0Bw0VXJKBgYPMS0J2VGIyWWlocms/edit?resourcekey=0-kTOcjGVz_hoqB_9vfexidA [Accessed 19.10.2021].

Nakamoto, S. (2008) Bitcoin: 'A Peer-to-Peer Electronic Cash System'. URL: https://bitcoin.org/bitcoin.pdf [Accessed 03.11.2021].

Nofer, M., Gomber, P., Hinz, O. (2017): 'Blockchain'. Bus Inf Syst Eng 59, pp. 183–187.

Qin, K., Zhou, L., Gamito, P., Jovanovic, P., Gervais, A. (2021a): 'An Empirical Study of DeFi Liquidations: Incentives, Risks, and Instabilities'. URL: https://arxiv.org/pdf/2106.06389.pdf [Accessed 29.10.2021].

Qin, K., Zhou, L., Livshits, B., Gervais, A. (2021b): 'Attacking the DeFi Ecosystem with Flash Loans for Fun and Profit'. In International Conference on Financial Cryptography and Data Security. Springer, Berlin, Heidelberg, pp. 3–32.

Perez, D., Werner, S., Xu, J., Livshits, B. (2021): Liquidations: DeFi on a Knife-edge. In Financial Cryptography and Data Security. URL: https://arxiv.org/pdf/2009.13235.pdf?utm_campaign=ConsenSys%20Diligence&utm_source=hs_email&utm_medium=email&_hsenc=p2ANqtz-9syjEr6eOfKaTzHLqmYJYnNrQbNAA4bYsCZamlMBjA8f65_pfvV8c35FsfKbtbtwByA6Ko [Accessed 02.11.2021].

Reinhart, C., Sbrancia, M. (2011): 'The liquidation of government debt'. In: Technical Report. National Bureau of Economic Research, Economic Policy, 30, pp. 291–333.

REQBIN (2021): 'Run Curl'. URL: https://reqbin.com/curl [Accessed 25.11.2021].

Roth, A.E. (2015): 'Who Gets What—and Why: The New Economics of Matchmaking and Market Design'. Houghton Mifflin Harcourt, New York.

Roth, J., Schär, F., Schöpfer, A. (2019): 'The Tokenization of Assets: Using Blockchains for Equity Crowdfunding'. URL: https://dx.doi.org/10.2139/ssrn.3443382 [Accessed 23.10.2021].

Saengchote, K. (2021): 'Decentralized lending and its users: Insights from Compound'. Discussion Papers 162, Puey Ungphakorn Institute for Economic Research, Bangkok.

Sauer, A. (1991): 'Die Bereinigung von Aktienkursen—Ein kurzer Überblick über Konzept und praktische Umsetzung'. Universität Karlsruhe (TH)—Deutsche Finanzdatenbank—DFDB.

Sherman, A., Javani, F., Zhang, H., Golaszewski, E. (2018): 'On the Origins and Variations of Blockchain Technologies'. University of Maryland, Baltimore County (UMBC).

Shleifer, A., Vishny, R. (1992): 'Liquidation values and debt capacity: A market equilibrium approach'. In: The Journal of Finance 47, 4, pp. 1343–1366.

Szabo, N. (1994): 'Smart Contracts'. URL: https://www.fon.hum.uva.nl/rob/Courses/InformationInSpeech/CDROM/Literature/LOTwinterschool2006/szabo.best.vwh.net/smart.contracts.html [Accessed 19.10.2021].

Szabo, N. (1997): 'The Idea of Smart Contracts'. URL: https://nakamotoinstitute.org/the-idea-of-smart-contracts/ [Accessed 19.10.2021].

Schär, F. (2021): 'Decentralized Finance: On Blockchain- and Smart Contract-Based Financial Markets'. Federal Reserve Bank of St. Louis Review, Second Quarter 2021, pp. 153-74.

Scheid, E., Hegnauer, T.; Rodrigues, B.; Stiller, B. (2019): 'Bifröst: a Modular Blockchain Interoperability API'. In: 44th Conference on Local Computer Networks (LCN 2019), Osnabrück, pp. 1–9.

Swan, Melanie. 2015. 'Blockchain: Blueprint for a New Economy'. O'Reilly Media, Sebastopol.

Swanson T. (2015): 'Consensus-as-a-service: a brief report on the emergence of permissioned, distributed ledger systems'. R3 CEV Work Pap. 04/2015.

Tara A., Ivkushkin K., Butean A., Turesson H. (2019): 'The Evolution of Blockchain Virtual Machine Architecture Towards an Enterprise Usage Perspective'. In Silhavy R. (eds)

'Software Engineering Methods in Intelligent Algorithms'. CSOC 2019. Advances in Intelligent Systems and Computing, vol 984. Springer, pp. 370–379.

Titman, S. (1984): 'The effect of capital structure on a firm's liquidation decision'. In: Journal of financial economics 13, 1, pp. 137–151.

Tolmach, P., Li, Y., Lin, S., Liu, Y. (2021): 'Formal Analysis of Composable DeFi Protocols'. In: 1st Financial Cryptography Workshops (2021), IFCA Conference.

Wang, Y., Chen, Y., Deng, S., Wattenhofer, R. (2021): 'Cyclic Arbitrage in Decentralized Exchange Markets'. URL: https://arxiv.org/pdf/2105.02784.pdf [Accessed 02.11.2021].

Werner, S., Perez, D., Gudgeon, L., Klages-Mundt, A., Harz, D., Knottenbelt, W. (2021): 'SoK: Decentralized Finance (DeFi)'. URL: https://arxiv.org/pdf/2101.08778v5.pdf [Accessed 22.10.2021].

Wong, E. (1977): 'Retrieving dispersed data from SDD-1: A system for distributed databases'. 1977 Berkeley Workshop on Distributed Data Management and Computer Networks, University of California, Berkeley, CA.

Wood, G. (2021): 'Ethereum: a secure decentralised generalised transaction ledger'. URL: https://ethereum.github.io/yellowpaper/paper.pdf [Accessed 19.10.2021].

Xu, L., Shah, N., Chen, L., Diallo, N., Gao, Z., Lu, Y., Shi. W. (2017): 'Enabling the sharing economy: Privacy respecting contract based on public blockchain'. In ACM Workshop on Blockchain, Cryptocurrencies and Contracts, pp. 15–21.

YCharts (2021): 'Ethereum Average Gas Price'. URL: https://ycharts.com/indicators/ethereum_average_gas_price [Accessed 02.11.2021].